C000175433

More Memories of Bristol

The publishers would like to thank the following companies for their support in the production of this book

Main Sponsor

Bailey Caravans Limited

Airbus UK

Badminton School

Bristol Old Vic Trust

Guilberts

Solomon Hare

Horeword Homewares

McBraida Plc

National Deposit Friendly Society Limited

Pattersons

C H Pearce Construction Limited

The Ray Engineering Company Limited

Redcliffe Magnatronics

Rexam Medical Packaging

Seetru Limited

Elizabeth Shaw

Thomas Silvey Limited

WTB Group

Western Power Distribution

Reece Winstone Archive & Publishing

First published in Great Britain by True North Books Limited
England HX5 9AE
01422 377977

ISBN 1 903204 43 7

Text, design and origination by True North Books Limited
Printed and bound by The Amadeus Press Limited

Introduction from Patrick Howard

The team of people who are Bailey of Bristol are delighted to be associated with the production of this book. As a major manufacturing company in the south of the city we know the quality of the people in this historic area.

When the company was founded in 1947, little did those pioneers realise the changes that would occur in Bristol in the next fifty or so years. Prior to the first world war the site on which we currently manufacture was an active brick-works, surrounded by the most northern of the Somerset coal mines - the miners cottages in the area are testament to this time. Before this period the area had been a Victorian rubbish tip, after the second world war it, reputedly, returned to this role, for a short time, as many of the blitz damaged Bristol tramways were dumped here.

From its beginnings and through many years of growth in the area, Bailey Caravans has seen many neighbours cease business for one reason or another. When the company recently gave a restored mid-fifties model to the Bristol Industrial Museum, at Princes Wharf it was parked amidst many a reminder of the diversity of the once great Bristol manufacturing base. Bailey are one of the few left to carry that torch forward.

The stories and photographs that follow show clearly the changes in architecture and fashion of the area. The picture cannot, however, impart the real and spirited heart of the people of Bristol. At Bailey, people, drawn predominantly from the area, continually strive to design, manufacture and market a better range of products. This is achieved following close consultation with the company's customers - thus developing a product that meets their needs at an affordable price. The reputation associated with the company and its products over its entire life is testament to the skills of the people who have made Bailey their chosen career.

The team at Bailey Caravans continue to grow and improve by the application of that famous philosophy "Shipshape and Bristol Fashion" - May we in the years to come continue on that path towards excellence.

Patrick Howard
Chairman

www.bailey-caravans.co.uk

Contents

Introduction

Come and walk with us as we head off on a journey down Memory Lane. In the pages of this new book we revisit the Bristol of our childhood, tread the pavements where we once played cowboys and Indians, and queue again for those cinema matinees where we cheered our screen heroes and jeered the longsuffering projectionist when the film broke, as it often did. We take a look back at the war-torn Bristol of our parents, and feel for them as they sheltered in terror, wondering whether the next bomb to fall would have their name on it, then got up and carried on as normal the following day, for these were people drawn together in the spirit of courage and camaraderie that only the tough times seem to induce.

Continuing our journey through time we stop and wonder at the city our grandparents knew well, when ships were able to tie up at St Augustine's bridge, and daredevil screen cowboy Tom Mix was a superstar - and when buildings, that were by the end of the 20th century replaced by glass, steel and concrete, still stood proud as well-known landmarks. Those were the days when men wore the trousers and women wore their flowered wrap-around aprons. They cooked meals, did the washing, cleaned the house and brought up children. If Granny went out to work at all, she earned her pin money in a male-dominated workplace. The Great War had brought slow change which was continued during World War II; it took the flower power of the 1960s to set mighty wheels rolling in the direction of women's liberation.

'More Memories of Bristol' is not a serious and pedestrian work of local history, detailing the progression of the city from Cabot's voyage to Newfoundland, through the notorious 'triangular' trading of the 18th century, to the devastation wrought by the air raids of the second world war. On the contrary this is a collection of delightful images of a living, breathing and working city, chronicling the dramatic changes brought about within living memory, each one enriched by text that is informative, thought provoking and humorous.

The residents of Allington Road celebrate VE Day.

Within the pages of the book you can relive the days when you lacquered your 'beehive' hair-do, donned your stiletto heels and 'twisted the night away' at the old Byzantine Granary, or rooted for your favourite riders at Knowle Stadium, drawn by the glorious thrill of speedway. Take a pleasant stroll with us through the Centre Gardens before they were replaced much more recently by rows of spouting fountains set in concrete, enormous masts and sails, and strange 'funnels' which light up at night. Look again at the once familiar streets and marvellous old buildings before the devastation brought about by bombing raids, and continued by the city planners of the 1950s and 60s. Revisit the old cinemas where you saw 'Kiss Me Kate' in 3D through those funny red and green cardboard spectacles. Remember how the realistic 3-dimensional effect made Kathryn Grayson and Howard Keel come alive? Then there was the wide-screen Cinemascope, another marvellous innovation of the 1950s. So many of Bristol's cinemas went eyes down to Bingo in a desperate attempt to survive the advent of the small screen in the corner of the lounge. Was the old Carlton, or the Metropole in Ashley Road, the scene, perhaps, of your first date?

We know that there can be no progress without change, but so much of the city has gone forever, and we mourn the loss of such edifices as the CWS building and its familiar clock against which we checked our watches, and the Sun Insurance building in the Centre, with its columns and dome; remember that huge sun motif with its golden rays, and the words which informed all who raised their eyes above shop window level that this was 'The oldest insurance office in the world'? Replaced now by soaring glass and concrete, like so many others.

Somewhere along the line, however, we have come to terms with our new city. Like a new pair of shoes in which we at first felt ill at ease, the passage of time has brought familiarity and even comfort. And the familiarity, of course, is ongoing. In fifty years or so, will a future generation of Bristolians campaign against the demolition of their heritage - those rows of spouting fountains, perhaps, or the Galleries Shopping Centre? Let's face it - which of us would want to be without our modern shopping

centres, where we can browse among the stores and meet friends for lunch without braving the winter wind and rain; the wide dual carriageways and multi-storey car parks, which address the problems faced by the 21st century motorist, or the vibrant waterside attractions and the thriving eating houses and businesses which have brought life once more to the city's wharves?

Bristol is still a city of contrasts. Side by side with our modern shops and centres of entertainment stand ancient inns, splendid churches, and old thoroughfares steeped in history. Thankfully, we can still tread the old route up the hillside we know as Christmas Steps; built as the merry monarch, King Charles II, was dallying with his pretty orange seller Nell Gwynne, and lined today by specialist shops and antique dealers, we can take a step back in time as we climb and browse among the whatnot stands and copper kettles of a bygone era - then wonder, as we reach the top, at the 15th century chapel of the Three Kings of Cologne, measuring just 18ft by 22ft.

We can still light a candle in Bristol's magnificent Cathedral, which began life as St Augustine's Abbey back in the year 1140 - and even attend a concert within its stately walls. And we can raise our eyes with justifiable pride to Brunel's masterpiece, the Clifton Suspension Bridge. Engineer in chief of the Great Western Railway, builder of Temple Meads Station, designer and engineer of the 'Great Western', the 'Great Britain' and the 'Great Eastern' - destined to be the biggest ship afloat for 40 years - Isambard Kingdom Brunel's genius is legendary. Unbelievably, he was just 24 years old when he designed the incredible suspension bridge which still soars above the 250ft deep Avon Gorge; sadly, his death at the age of 53 prevented him from seeing the completion of his masterpiece.

With a noble heritage to build on as well as a great future to look forward to, Bristol has to be one of the most exciting places in which to live. History is still in the making! So relax in your armchair, turn the clock back to the days of your youth, and enjoy a whole world of nostalgia as you leaf through the pages of 'More Memories of Bristol'.

Around the city centre

The red pen of the city planners took over where the wartime air raids left off, and Bristol lost many of its surviving fine buildings in what the novelist J B Priestley once labelled 'Council vandalism'. Readers will perhaps remember the chemists Strode Cosh & Penfold and James Phillips furnishers in this shot of Union Street, captured in the late 1940s. The stores on the left fell victim to the redevelopment of the area, and in time were replaced by the Tesco Metro store, while the right eventually saw the building of the Galleries Shopping Centre. Beyond the Nelson Street and Broad Mead crossing, Broadmead Baptist Church can be seen in the distance on the right towards Horse Fair. Few things were sacred - even churches - and Broadmead Chapel, too, was demolished in the late 1960s and replaced by shops. Union Street is, of course, now part of Bristol's one-way system; as we can see, vehicles travelled in both directions at the time of the photograph. There was little traffic movement on the day (all parked and gone to the Odeon, perhaps?), and a lone cyclist makes his way towards us against today's traffic flow.

By the autumn of 1940 Britain had been at war for a year. Along with most other everyday commodities, petrol was strictly rationed - though who would think it, judging by the stream of traffic in College Green on this sunny day? Bristol, with the rest of the country, was preparing for air raids. With the street lighting gone for the duration of the war and headlights of all vehicles shaded, driving in the blackout was tricky, as our more mature readers will remember. Many drivers resorted to painting the wings, front and rear bumpers and running-boards of their cars white in an attempt to avoid accidents - though many accidents did still happen. Note the shop windows on the far left, which have been taped over to minimise the effects of flying glass during an air raid, and the pedestrians dutifully carrying their gas masks. The tops of buses, normally painted white, were blackened during the war as camouflage during air raids. Even in wartime, normal life went on, however, and in the background, work in the Centre continues on covering the River Frome. But very soon after this photograph was captured, the air raids were to become a grim reality.

Above and right: So many changes! These views of Colston Avenue as it was in September 1949 will stir many memories - and perhaps renew a few sighs as we remember the lovely old buildings which survived the war only to fall victim to modernisation. On the corner of Clare Street a row of sun blinds protects the goodies in the window of

Thornton's Chocolate Kabin; the elegant Sun building with its ornate columns and dome was destined to become the site for a tall office block. Nearby, the Dunlop building, which still had its unusual tower at the time of the photograph, was in time to become the Watershed Arts complex. Across the Centre Gardens, the bus company's booking offices still wore their 'olde worlde' look at the time of the photograph; it has now lost its impressive Tudor effect, though the clock remains. Spot the statue of Edmund Burke on the left. Is the great man directing the traffic? Or has he been picked up and placed on the ridge tiles of the public conveniences in the foreground? The angle of a shot can bring a smile to our faces. Burke's qualities as a social reformer were not recognised during his time as a Bristol MP in the late 1770s - the city was not ready for this forward thinker. His statue was erected 100 years later.

Top right: A sight to bring the old memories flooding back to our more mature readers - an old horse-drawn vehicle clopping through the centre of Bristol. There is little traffic about in the Centre in this memorable view, and the cyclist calmly hogging the middle of the road in the days long before cycle helmets were required, would appear to be in little danger. He is approaching the notorious 'scissors crossing' caused by

a merging of traffic, well remembered by Bristol motorists - especially those who merged more firmly than they intended, and suffered dented wings and smashed headlights! In 1957 this large traffic island was removed to bring an end to the problem. Readers may well have checked their watches by the clock on the old CWS building, a landmark which was also doomed to be replaced by a modern block - albeit still with a clock. Adverts, too, belong to the city's history, and the massive Table Waters sign by 'you know who' was part of our scenery for years. The Schweppes company took advantage of the spy fever that was raging in the 1960s, and those 'you know who' adverts made William Franklyn, who acted in various spoof spy situations, familiar to every household that owned a television set.

A panorama of memories. It's when we see such a vista, captured from the University Tower in 1957, that we realise just how much the city has lost, either to Nazi bombs or to modernisation. Fry's factory - seen on the far left - survived the war unscathed, and its 220ft chimney was one of Bristol's most familiar landmarks until the building was demolished in 1961. The long building nearer to us is Electricity House. The spires and towers of many churches point heavenwards in this view: on the left behind Electricity House is St John's of the Wall; further to the right, St Peter's, then St Mary le Port - both bombed during the war; moving on, the tall spire of Christ Church; All Saints; St Nicholas, destroyed by enemy bombs; Holy Cross, seen on the right near Temple Meads goods station, also bombed; the church of St Thomas a Beckett, now closed, lies nearby, and nearer to us we see the elegant tower of St Stephens, with the offices of the Evening World nearby. St Mary's on the Quay is just off-centre in the foreground. Trenchard Street cuts across the view from the right corner; the YMCA was later to replace some of these old buildings. Redevelopment would in future years transform the foreground of this view with new housing.

Above: How many of our readers once rocked the night away in the old Byzantine granary? Remember those dances back in the 60s and 70s, and the marvellous music with a beat that stirred the blood and had us twisting to Chubby Checker tunes and rocking to the music made popular by the Rolling Stones and Status Quo? With a little persuasion, a few may even admit to having seen The Ladybirds in the far off days of their reckless youth. They were a lively girl band whose particular attraction is perhaps best left unmentioned.... The old granary was a fortunate survivor among the many buildings in Bristol which fell victim to the city planners, and has even been used in the popular TV series 'Only Fools and Horses'. Llandoger Trow, an old inn nearby in King Street, also survived. Welsh Back, whose name reminds us of the trade which once flourished between Bristol and South Wales, was one of the city's earliest quays. The waterside, of course, was a prime target for the Nazi bombs, and during the second world war this area, once alive with warehouses and shipping, was laid waste. Modern office blocks have brought the waterside to life once more. Left of centre in this view, which dates from 31st May 1957, spot the Memorial dedicated to merchant seamen.

Right: It was a busy day in the Centre when this scene was recorded by the camera in the spring of 1940, and the white bumper bars and kerbstones, painted to make them more visible in the blackout, emphasise the fact that this was wartime. But wartime or not, the scheduled construction work went on just the same. Note the small crowd of people on the far right of the picture; they are watching builders working on the covering in of the River Frome. There is no sign of it today, but from the 13th century a lively quay had reached into the city as far as Colston Avenue. Work on culverting the river had begun in 1936, and four years on it was nearing completion. Note, too, the tram lines which still remained in the centre. A decision had been made during the early 1930s that all trams should disappear from the city by the end of the decade; the war changed things, and the old trams hung on in parts of the city until 1941. Covering tram track with tarmac was not on Bristol's agenda, and removal of some tramlines for their scrap value began as early as 1939, causing regular traffic tailbacks.

Below: The Tower of St Mary Redcliffe is the vantage point that gives us this peep at Bristol as it was in the mid 1950s. Looking up Redcliffe Hill - today a wide dual carriageway - towards Bedminster, a number of long vanished and sadly half-forgotten landmarks draw our eye: to the right of centre in the distance, the old Zion Chapel, today the Area Housing Office, and to the right of that, WD & HO Wills' factory, which once provided employment in the tobacco industry for thousands of Bristolians, and would make way for the Asda superstore. It was the Wills family whose generosity helped to found Bristol University. Insurance offices would one day replace the parade of shops on the right. Remember the faggot shop, whose chitterlings were to die for? And the old Ship Inn? All gone. Pets' Paradise, at the far end of the row of shops, would supply your pets with baskets, collars, leads, and anything else to do with feeding, rearing and training them. The store relocated to Victoria Street but later closed down. New housing had been a priority in Bristol since the heavy losses of the second world war, and the first of the new flats can be seen on the left; the Redcliffe flats were yet to be built across the road.

Above: The old Broadmead Baptist Church, which would later be redeveloped, was still with us when this scene was captured back in 1955. Behind the church we can see the scaffolding of the new Lewis's store which was being built at the time, and further back, the spire of the Welsh Congregational Church. The spire, too, was to be demolished a few years on, when it was found to be unsafe.

The camera recorded a quiet day in Lower Union Street, and there was little movement except for half a dozen pedestrians going about their business. Two out of the three parked cars are of the old, 'sit up and beg' design. This was the mid 50s, however, and car design was poised on the brink of dramatic change. Headlights would be faired-in and incorporated into sleeker body lines, running boards would vanish, flashing indicators would replace the semaphore type (remember how easy it was to forget them and leave them sticking out?), and even quarter-light windows would gradually disappear from our cars. At the time of the photograph Britain was well on the way towards post-war prosperity, and car ownership, once an unattainable dream, was fast becoming a reality in many households.

Top: Peace had come to Bristol after six long years of war, and these buildings in Queen's Road, pictured in November 1946, had managed to survive the worst of the bombing raids. Traffic, you will notice, ran in both directions at the time. The names above the shops on the left will ring many bells among our older readers who will remember Fortts, whose delivery van stands at the ready, Lalondes estate agents, Bristol Wireless, and Brights' department store. Bristol Wireless, who advertised themselves as 'wireless and TV specialists', were established in Bristol back in 1922. Brights were to be taken over by the House of Frazer, become Dingles - and eventually close their doors at the end of the 20th Century. And remember Buxton's chemists shop? Their canopy can be seen on the opposite side of the road. This was the place to go, not only to have your doctor's medicines dispensed but to buy the popular home remedies that had stood the test of time. Buxton's were a little more specialist than most 'run of the mill' chemists, however, as alongside their provision of conventional medication and home remedies, they dispensed homeopathic treatments to those who preferred to treat their ailments without the use of drugs.

Below: There are few signs of festivity in this view of Merchant Street, captured back in 1959, where reconstruction is still in progress in the background. Yet the date was 21st December, and with three more shopping days left before the big day, everyone, from this police officer on point duty to the small boy in short trousers, would have Christmas - and presents, either buying or receiving them - on their minds. Most of the ladies caught on camera have their shopping bags and carriers, and no doubt the contents include gifts and the odd Christmas pudding! It was during the 1950s that post-war prosperity began to make a difference in many households, who found that money - and the consumer goods to buy with it - was more plentiful than a decade earlier. But even so, Christmas was far less commercialised than today, when decorations, cards, and Christmas trees find their way into the stores around the end of September. By Guy Fawkes' night every shop you enter glitters with tinsel and fairy lights, and the yearly foot slog begins as we search for the latest over priced computer game, or a cardigan for Aunt Annie in exactly the right shade of blue.

Right: Through all the changing scenes of life... there is little we can do except accept them. By 1966, changes on a small scale - and on the large - were well advanced in Bristol. From the closing down of small shops such as Maynards, where we used to buy our midget gems and liquorice allsorts, to the opening of pizza, kebab, and other fast food outlets in the Centre, constant change is here to stay. Postwar university buildings - the schools of Engineering, Chemistry and Medicine - shape the skyline, with the Royal Fort jutting up halfway along. Many readers will remember the construction of these new centres of learning - and the building of the ugly chimney of Kingsdown boiler house. How many watched the chimney being delivered, slowly and carefully, by Wynns of Horfield Road, with tractors fore and aft? The Hippodrome, as important a part of Bristol's history as any other, has, by the date of the photograph, lost its familiar globe and its upper storey; the theatre remains an important entertainments centre. Colston Hall, to the rear of the Wessex coaches booking office, is also thankfully still with us. Traffic flow has changed since 1966, the north side being two way and the south side buses only (and anyone else who can get away with it!).

Far right: An image to remind us, perhaps, of the simple, uncommercialised Christmases of our childhood, when the festive season meant rather more than parties, presents, and acute indigestion! You may be familiar with the story of the harrassed young mum with a fractious toddler in tow who paused at the crib in her shopping centre to read the words below: 'Glory to God in the highest.' 'They're even bringing religion into Christmas now,' she was heard to mutter as she moved on. Year by year, the festive season moves further from its

Christian origins. But the lighted Christmas tree in College Green back in 1958 provides a beautiful backdrop to this scene of the very first Christmas, and mothers have brought their children to gaze in wonder at the crib, and the young mother Mary and her child, the son of God whose first home was a stable and whose bed was a manger. The crib served to remind passers by that though they might not count themselves well to do, there were many in the city who could only look forward to a very lean Christmas. Gifts were being collected on the day of the photograph to pass on to children who would otherwise be forgotten by Santa.

A pleasant way to spend an hour or two on a sunny April day! Whether your seat was a wooden 'park' bench or simply the low wall bordering the now non existent flower beds, lingering in Broad Quay with the sun on your face was one of life's simple pleasures as Spring bloomed again after a long, cold winter. And if you had your lunch box with you, so much the better. Were the seagulls as rapacious back in 1958, we wonder - or have they only acquired in recent years the unpleasant trick of snatching the sandwich, pasty or chips from your hand? All seemed well, however, on this bright Wednesday morning, and every available seat in the semicircle around the Neptune statue appears to be filled. The Centre is an area which has been transformed almost beyond recognition since the late 1950s; only Neptune remains constant - and his situation has undergone some dizzying changes in his long life. Cast in lead, the ancient Roman 'god of the sea' was installed, together with his own fountain, in Temple Street back in 1723. After a number of moves, in 1949 Neptune was given a permanent home and a granite plinth at St Augustine's bridgehead.

At leisure

A sight we will never see again - a ship tied up at St Augustine's Bridge! This charming photograph dates from June 1935, a year before work began on covering in this stretch of the River Frome. The equipment may have changed, but an ice cream seller was as popular then as now, and an indulgent grandad has dipped into his pocket and bought his little grandaughter an ice cream cone. The view captures the Hippodrome, boasting a generous 'three hours programme'. The establishment was well justified in advertising itself as 'Bristol's centre of entertainment'. Built as a variety theatre, the Hippodrome was massive, with a luxurious 2,000 seat auditorium with stalls, circle and gallery, and a state-of-the-art dome which could be opened for ventilation. By 1930, however, the lure of moving pictures was beginning to outpace live theatre, and after the runaway success of an experimental 2-week showing of 'Congorilla', the Hippodrome dedicated itself wholly to the 'silver screen' in September 1932. Six years later, however, it showed its last film and bravely returned to live theatre. Its stage was later extended to accommodate successful West End shows, and the theatre remains highly popular today.

Above: A trestle table set up on an old bomb site and a talent for fast talking that would attract the punters; these were the basic ingredients for earning yourself a bob or two on the side. And if, added to that, you had a pack of cards in your pocket and an aptitude for sleight of hand, your success was guaranteed. 'Find the lady' may well have been the game in progress here in Fairfax Street back in 1955. It looked easy: keep your eye fixed on the queen, note where the man put it, and put your money on one of the three cards. Then, unbelievably, he would turn up the five of clubs or some other card and say, 'Unlucky, sir - you missed out there.' Your money was whisked away and you were left wondering how in the world you could have been mistaken; after all, you had actually seen the queen as he placed it on the table! It was clever stuff, and drawing a crowd was simple. A couple of mates standing around to win a game or two would swiftly pull in others to watch and see how easy it was to gain a little extra cash. The three card trick was not the only other game around - Crown and Anchor, played with dice, was another way to lose your hard-earned cash. All illegal, of course - but fun to watch!

Watched by a huge crowd of supporters, the four riders at Knowle Speedway are off. The size of the crowd could possibly point to this being a championship match - unfortunately we have no record. Riders competed against each other in a championship, whereas normally the four riders represented two opposing teams.
Poised for action in the background are the team of mechanics, ready for any eventuality. An ambulance was also usually present; in this dangerous sport injuries and even fatalities have been known, as the author of these words can verify, having been present at a fatal speedway accident in the early 1950s.

During the 1930s, the thrill of speed drew fans in their hundreds to Knowle Stadium to watch speedway, rooting for their favourite riders. Perhaps you and your friends were sometimes among the crowd? The view from the front few rows was brilliant - but the cinders could hit you and sting like hornets as they spat viciously from the bike wheels on every circuit. The greyhound racing track was a popular attraction at Knowle Stadium long before speedway was introduced in the late 1930s. The open fields of Whitchurch and Hartcliffe, which form the background of this fascinating photograph, have since been developed as a residential area.

Above: An image to give us all a trip down Memory Lane - the Saturday matinee where, for just a few coppers, we could see one of the popular cartoons, a couple of feature films, and exciting trailers of forthcoming films to entice us back time and again. Roy Rogers and his faithful Trigger; the Lone Ranger; Superman; the dog Lassie - they were all there. And remember those 'cliffhanger' serials which left the hero tied up in the path of a circular saw, where he remained for a nailbiting week until the following Saturday? The whole programme was punctuated by cheers and jeers, flying bits of rubbish, the popping of bubble gum, the 'oohs' of excitement, and the shouts of 'Put a penny in!' that harassed the long suffering projectionist when the film broke, as frequently happened. All very thrilling stuff.

The Carlton cinema in Westbury on Trym was a popular cinema in its day, and its 820 seat auditorium was often well filled, a ground level cafe adding to its appeal. 'The Reluctant Debutante' was being screened at the time of the photograph. The days of the old Carlton were already numbered, however; it was pictured here in April 1959 not long before it closed and the site was later redeveloped as Westbury's new shopping centre.

Remember the old Metropole in Ashley Road - the scene, perhaps, of your first date? Its doors were closed at the time of the photograph, 28th March 1959 - a Saturday - and the few pedestrians caught by the camera are more preoccupied with their shopping than with the cinema. Once an unpretentious little picture house, extensive building work and renovation in 1938 turned the Metropole into an impressive modern cinema which could comfortably seat 1,460 people. The 1930s and 40s were, of course, the heyday of the cinema, but by the 1950s audiences were falling drastically. In 1968 the Metropole went 'eyes down' to bingo, a game believed by many at first to be one of those crazes that come along from time to time, enjoy immense popularity, then fade once more into obscurity. But marking off 'Heath's den, Number 10' or those 'two little ducks', followed, on rare occasions, by the excitement of needing that very last number - and the final triumph of being able to shout 'House!', proved to be addictive. Over the years bingo turned out to be no flash in the pan, and with big money prizes on offer the game remains popular today.

Top: If there had been a competition for the most beautifully decorated street in the days leading up to the Coronation of King George VI, surely Bishop Street would have been in with an excellent chance. Bishop Street, a modest street off Whitehouse Street (an area which was to suffer heavy bombing during World War II), would normally have been buzzing with life. Every door, however, has been closed and the inhabitants tidied away to display the Coronation preparations at their best. Even the dustbins have been placed neatly outside each house for the benefit of the camera. Younger readers may not perhaps be aware that the coronation celebrations held on 12th May 1937 did not follow the original plan. In the event the monarch being crowned was not Edward VIII, who Britain had expected to reign after the death of King George V, but his younger brother George VI. When the King abdicated after 325 days to marry American divorcee Wallis Simpson, however, Prince Albert was catapulted into the kingship he had no training for and did not want. But he did his duty and bravely took up the reins, adopting the title George VI. He and his wife Elizabeth - parents of our Queen - became King and Queen of England.

Above: Bunting, garlands and flags decorating Castle Street tell us that a special event is taking place, and this festive occasion was 'British-French Week', which was staged at the beginning of June 1930. The carnival atmosphere has tempted crowds of people into the city centre, and strangely the great majority of them appear to be men, who are all wearing hats or caps, without which they would hesitate to be seen out of doors. Dress code was far more formal in the first half of the 20th century. In spite of the fact that only one vehicle is visible in the far distance, a very smart police officer holds up his hand to direct what would appear at first glance to be non-existent traffic. Foster Bros are holding a sale, and with shirts on offer at only 2/6d, the proprietors must be hoping that the special event would bring in the customers by the dozen. These shirts, which cost just twelve and a half pence in today's currency, may appear to us to have been virtually given away. But remember that in 1930 Britain was going through a slump; average wages were just over £2 a week, and many men had actually taken a cut in pay!

Both pictures: It was 8th May 1945, and Churchill and Truman had declared VE Day. The war in Europe was over, and it was party time in Bristol. There were few communities around the city who did not hold a party for the local children, and this one was organised by the residents of Allington Road, Southville. Doing the best they could with the ingredients they could get hold of or had carefully hoarded for such an occasion, the mothers standing in the background (of the picture above) managed to conjure up sandwiches, cake, buns and even jelly to give the children a rare treat. Flowers adorn the table, union jacks and bunting hang on the walls, best clothes are the order of the day - and the tot on the right has been given a 'Shirley Temple' hair-do to mark the occasion. Fathers as well as mothers have worked together to give the kids a day to remember. While providing the food was still recognised as 'women's work' at the time, the menfolk would have provided the muscle power behind the placing of the tables and benches - and perhaps organised a few races and team games. In the end it was all worth waiting for, and the 'V for victory' sign reveals the upbeat atmosphere (left).

The children pictured here look well fed and happy, but they had grown up on a basic diet that held few sweets or luxuries. Clothing, too, was rationed, and people had to 'make do and mend' whenever they could; by the end of the war most women's wardrobes were looking decidedly tired. Everyone was looking forward to the future, to a time when they could stop using tinned dried eggs, and shop for clothes without counting how many coupons they had. It was to be a long wait. Clothing was rationed until 1949, and sweets until 1953 - and in fact bread went on ration in 1946! It was 1954 before all rationing in Britain was ended. Brand names once more appeared on certain food products, and young people were amazed to realise that products such as margarine could be labelled as Stork or Summer County instead of just being plain old foul tasting margarine. Was it really made from whale oil?

Left: Delighted crowds gave Sir Winston Churchill a rousing welcome when he became Chancellor of Bristol University on 21st June 1946, and the camera captured the moment for posterity as he approached the Great Door, followed by his daughter Mary and accompanied by the Vice-Chancellor Philip Morris (afterwards Sir Philip). By that time the war had been over for a year, but the great wartime hero who had promised Britain little more than 'blood, sweat and tears' still had great pulling power; his stirring speeches had been an inspiration during the war, and the wide smiles on virtually every face in the crowd say it all: the people loved him. It had been Churchill's strong leadership which had taken the

country through the bitter years of loss and hardship to decisive victory - and perhaps without him, Britain would have surrendered to Hitler. Born in 1874, Churchill joined the army, fighting in Cuba, India and in Egypt with Kitchener. A war correspondent in the Boer War, he was captured, but escaped - with a price on his head - to England. He entered politics, became a junior minister in 1906, First Lord of the Admiralty in 1911, and wartime premier in 1940. A great soldier, statesman, author and artist, Winston Churchill died in 1965 at the age of 90.

Above: There's nothing like a marching band to set your foot tapping, and the crowds turned out in full force to watch this military parade on 4th June 1942. During the war processions were part and parcel of life. They were a recognised morale-booster, making the average person in the street feel in touch with the progress of the war, and the sound of an approaching band brought people to their doors and children running to join in. (Spot the kiddies marching along behind the seamen in this photograph.) Behind them, a Corporation Electricity Department lorry has been adorned with bunting and flags to mark the occasion. What a pity we don't know what the occasion was!

In the background we can pick out the Central Hotel and Baker Baker & Co's gaily striped blinds. All vastly different today, of course, apart from the Lord Mayor's Chapel on the far right, which thankfully survived the second world war. St Mark's has a very long history, and though it has been refurbished at intervals, much of it dates back to the 13th century. This beautiful Chapel - the only church in Britain which is owned by a local authority - remains a church which is very much alive today.

Above right: How many people would turn out today to view the moving of a statue? But this was March 1953, and the statue was rather special. Bristol had not taken kindly to the earlier removal of Queen Victoria's statue from College Green to a traffic roundabout, and a public campaign followed which brought the people and the city's Planning and Public Works Committee to a nose to nose confrontation. Happily, public opinion won the day and preparations went ahead to return the great monarch to what was seen as her rightful position. Large crowds assembled in College Green to watch the delicate operation as Her Majesty, with thick ropes tied around her royal middle, was lowered on to her plinth. Interestingly, a sealed bottle was buried beneath the statue containing current newspapers and coins which had been struck to commemorate the coronation of Queen Elizabeth II, which was due to take place three months later, along with a similar hoard which had been buried in 1888 when the statue was first erected. The Lord Mayor, Ald. V J Ross, supervised the ceremony along with Ald. W H Hennessy, who was Chairman of the Planning & Public Works Committee. During the early 1990s Queen Victoria underwent a further move, though the statue remained in College Green.

Above: 'I can't see, Dad!' Can't you almost hear the children begging to be lifted on to Dad's shoulders? And the cause of all the excitement? Tom Mix - every child's hero - was in town, booked to appear in a variety show at the Hippodrome, and nobody was going to miss his publicity parade through the streets of Bristol - even if they had to climb on to Neptune's statue to see him! The date was 5th March 1939, and the Hollywood superstar of those 1920s silent films was still wowing his audiences. Those who are old enough to remember them will recall the thrill they felt when stuntrider Mix galloped in to see off the outlaws on his faithful horse Tony - and the cinema would echo with the children's cheers and shouts. And remember those games of cowboys and Indians, when every boy wanted to be Tom Mix rounding up the rustlers in Dead Man's Gulch? It was Mix's daredevil stunts that roller-coastered him from the more mundane occupation of deputy marshall back in his home town, Dewey, to fame, fortune and international stardom. He was the hero of many adventure films, including 'North of Hudson Bay' (1924) and 'The Last Trail' (1927). The stuff that great memories are made of.

A staggering 20,000 people turned out to welcome the Queen and Prince Philip when they paid a visit to Bristol on 17th April 1956, and although the royal train was not due at Temple Meads until 10 o'clock, many had already staked their claim to a good view outside St Mary Redcliffe Church three hours earlier. The young and pretty Queen, who had been crowned just three years earlier, had been seen many times on television and in cinema newsreel. But film is far from the real thing, and Bristolians were eager to see the Queen and the Duke of Edinburgh for themselves. The children from Temple Colston or St Mary Redcliffe schools had a 'front row' view as the royal couple passed by on their way into the church (were you one of them?). It was a busy day for the visitors as they were whisked from place to place: Albion Dockyard, Charles Hill's shipyards; a naval inspection - then the official opening of the new Council House. Our photograph shows the Queen, who has, of course, been given flowers, with the Lord Mayor, Ald. H Crook, on Broad Quay, while behind her the Duke chats with the lucky VIPs.

The joys of the open road, Bailey-style

It sometimes happens that a chance remark or random event can change the course of someone's life radically, a person can make a passing observation which turns someone's thoughts in a completely different direction. This was certainly the case for Martin Bailey, founder of the market leading caravan manufacturers based at South Liberty Lane, Bristol.

Martin had been employed as a sheet metal worker with Bristol Aircraft Co. during the days of the second world war and though he didn't realise it at the time this was to prove to be extremely significant for his future. Later he turned his attention to cabinet making, producing Utility Furniture, which as those who were setting up home in the immediate aftermath of the war will remember only too well, was available in exchange for precious coupons; it also came with a choice - take it or leave it. Though it was designed with simplicity and functionality in view, the quality was usually of a high standard, produced as it was with a view to serving the needs of those young couples for a substantial part of their married lives. It may not have looked beautiful but items of this type of furniture are still in everyday use long after the cheaper flatpacks, which came later, have fallen to pieces.

Right: *The board of Bailey Caravans, (from left to right) Ceri Davies (Production Director), Stephen Howard (Director), Simon Howard (Marketing Director), Nigel Mattfield (Managing Director), Nick Howard (Technical Director), Patrick Howard (Chairman), Mike Bye (Financial Director) and John Parker (Sales Director).* ***Below:*** *Olympia Caravan Show, 1950s.*

In the end the caravan was sold at auction at the 'City Ground' for the princely sum of £200. This was 1948 - he never looked back.

The earliest advertisement for a Bailey caravan appeared in The Caravan in November that year. It reads as follows: The Saint adds another string to his harp, The Bailey Minor. Full headroom. Customers over 7 ft supplied with aspirin tablets. Really waterproof - if it leaks we'll shoot the makers. Springs in every bed - one for Ma, one for Dad, and two in reserve. Everything for £495 including insulation, jockey wheel, wine cellar and kettle. Even the Terror of Taplow would live happily in this van. Becketts of Bromsgrove and Becketts Enterprises of Felton and Boroughbridge were the earliest companies to act as distributors.

The latest season's range has been developed using a combination of over fifty years of experience in caravan manufacture and design with the latest production technology to attain new heights in touring home quality and style.

Bailey now have a formidable reputation for setting the standards in the industry, a reputation which has been further enhanced by the recent receipt of numerous product awards, including the prestigious Caravan Club 'Tourer of the Year Award' presented to the Bailey Pageant Imperial model.

The 2001 season consisted of a line-up of nineteen models from the Ranger, Pageant and Senator marques, each offering all the qualities for which Bailey touring homes have become renowned, not least of which remains outstanding value for money. Each new Bailey touring caravan complies with

Top left: *The Bailey workforce in 1960.*
Above left and Below: *Two Bailey caravans from the 1960s the 'Montane' (below) and the 'Maestro Continental'.*

Martin was working from Bedminster Down Road at the time in a building which was known as the 'Old School House', but which had also served as a fire station at one time. He was approached by a friend who wanted to buy some plywood (which was rationed in those difficult days after the war). He intended to build a caravan with this and Martin, seizing this wonderful business opportunity immediately responded by saying that he could build one too.

So he sat down with his business associate, a pencil and pad of paper in front of him, scratched his head, and set about designing the first of a long line of touring caravans. He was concerned to make it as practical, convenient and comfortable as possible. He always kept the needs of the purchaser at the forefront of his mind as he made the specification for his first model. Designing and building his prototype took six months of hard work, including one or two sleepless nights. His experience with sheet metal as well as his woodworking skills stood him in good stead and he was able to set about producing a caravan without having to recourse to outside help. Working entirely alone using only the hand tools, presses and glues with which he had formerly crafted pieces of furniture he at length proudly brought his brain-child to completion.

stringent European Quality standards and comes with a three year factory backed warranty to give the purchaser complete confidence in the product.

But things did not suddenly arrive at this present stage all at once. The growth of the business was steady but sure. Martin remained for a further 12 years at his original site at which time he was rapidly running out of adequate space. He started the search for a suitably larger site and found it in 1960 on South Liberty Lane, in the middle of the firm's present day site.

The business was in the fortunate position of having a well-designed product on the market just at the time when demand for it was about to take off. Caravans were practically unheard of for the average family before the second world war, but the mood of greater optimism evident after its end and especially after the end of rationing in the early 1950s meant that the day of the caravan had arrived. Over the next twenty years or so, the perception of the car changed from being an item for the wealthy few to something which was within the reach of thousands of 'ordinary' folk.

This coupled with a programme of road improvements undertaken by successive governments made the possibility of travelling around the country without the need to book in at hotels or guest houses very attractive, representing an economical way of taking the family for a few days away. In the words of a Bailey advert from around the mid 1970s, a Bailey caravan provides, 'the opportunity of taking a break, long or short, at any time you choose. The freedom to go your own way, at your own pace - free from the restraints of rigid preplanned timetables and destinations. Weekends suddenly become holidays when you can take off to the country or coast with the family. Holidays can be taken anywhere at home or abroad without months of

Left: *A Caravan Show in Switzerland circa 1967.*
Below: *Earls Court 1968.*

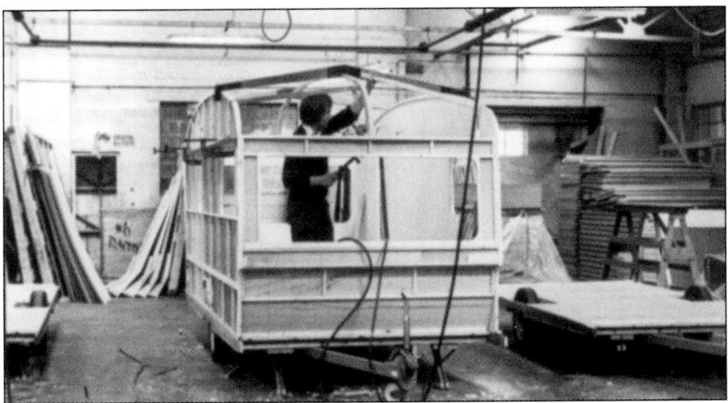

advance planning. And you can do it all in total comfort - in a Bailey caravan.'

Further developments followed, stimulated by the popularity of caravan owning. 1973 saw the introduction of caravan racing. Baileys found this a very exciting prospect and viewed it as a challenge that they had not come up against before. Baileys had always been regarded as a stable towing caravan and they had just launched a new range called Prima. With the help of many friends and acknowledging that the caravan was only part of the outfit consisting of the trailer itself and the car which was towing it, their efforts were rewarded with instant success. In the autumn of 1973 both Bailey and Prima caravans gained success at Silverstone with a Prima van winning the overall award.

Then in 1974 the Repco Brake Company sponsored the first ever Caravan Racing Championship. A good team had been established and all concerned were learning fast, through experimentation, the demands that caravan racing put on both car and caravan.

During that summer a prototype was developed from the experience that had been gained which was to prove an outright winner and give the company much information on which to base their next range of caravans. This is illustrated by the fact that the prototype, with all things equal, cornered at 10 miles an hour faster than the original racing caravan.

In June 1974 Andrew Higton driving a Vauxhall saloon car towing a Bailey caravan did the record lap of the Silverstone course in 1 min 35.2 sec at an average speed of 61.50 mph. Real benefits were passed on to Bailey customers in the form of many modifications which improved the design and performance of Bailey products. But, as they say, 'don't try this at home'.

It was around this time that Bailey after a short period in the hands of an engineering company was back in family ownership - the Howard family, members of which are still at the helm.

Bailey of Bristol is now in the enviable position of selling every model they can produce, such is the reputation for reliability, comfort and quality which the firm has built up over the years. In fact they could probably sell even more than the present production capacity permits. The company designs and manufactures a product which is regarded as the market leader, by user and retailer alike and it is their proud

This Page: *Stages in the production of Bailey Caravans from the 1970s.*

claim that when you see a Bailey on the road, you see a family enjoying itself.

A significant factor in the attractiveness of the Bailey range is their lightweight build. The feature developed in response to car manufacturers producing lighter-weight cars in the interests of fuel efficiency. And it is not only in the production of tourers that the company is prepared to stand ahead of the field. Their 1995 company brochure drew gasps of astonishment from press and customers - Bailey had taken the bold step of using black and white photography throughout, even on the brochure's cover. The effect was incredibly classy, totally in keeping, therefore, with the Bailey image as a whole.

There are now also successful markets on the continent for Bailey caravans. A network of around a dozen dealers was set up in Holland and a fledgling market operates in New Zealand.

Bailey caravans are made and sold from the Bristol South Liberty Lane site and through a network of 56 retailers extending across the whole of the UK. Retailers provide valuable feedback about customer requirements and these form the basis of refinements in the design and are the springboard for further innovative design concepts . Bailey are always seeking to provide what the customer wants, and

Left: *Colston Williams and Den Perrett celebrating 25 years service in 1976, Den retired in 1999 and Colston will retire in 2001.* ***Below:*** *The original South Liberty Lane site.*

the order book would indicate that that is certainly what they are managing to achieve.

The reason that many choose a Bailey for their first caravan, and why also many families return to them when they want to update their present model is because of the reputation, sustained over many years of the Bailey functional design, the excellence of the materials used, reliability, the lightweight construction and above all superb value for money they represent.

An important watershed in the history of the firm came in 1996 with the introduction of the pioneering Rangers - fully equipped, quality touring caravans with prices pitched below the £10,000 threshold. Over 1100 of them were sold in that year alone.

Ease of towing is a well-regarded feature of Bailey caravans, and the purchaser can rely on continued support from the firm long after he has signed on the dotted line to purchase a model. The sales team recognise that a caravan is a significant investment for any family and they seek to offer efficient and prompt after sales service, ensuring that no one is likely to regret ever acquiring one of the Bailey products. The level of stock in the spares department is considerable and every effort is made to meet a customer's need in the shortest possible time.

Bailey Owners Club has over 500 members throughout the country and holds at least 60 rallies a year. Most of them are held in the UK but other locations have been used from time to time. Sites for rallies vary considerably from a simple field with a tap and perhaps a barbecue, to more sophisticated events with a dance hall and band.

It is company policy to continually improve their understanding of their customers needs and to provide

Top: *A staff photograph in April 1978.*
Above left: *The Bailey 'Prima', 1973.*
Below: *A Bailey 'Maestro' being lifted into the new trade showroom and training centre in 1983.*

the most competitive products and services on their behalf. They have now risen to be the third biggest manufacturer of caravans in the UK, they intend to take the lead for product developments from expressed wishes of the user rather then on ease of production. At Bailey the customer is king.

Just about everything that can be changed has changed at Bailey since 1948. The way a van is put together is one of them. Whereas Martin used his own strength and hand tools in the beginning, these days state-of-the-art machinery ensures accurate and cost-effective methods of manufacture are used for Bailey products.

The company regard themselves as 'timber engineers'. Nowadays precision CNC machines, CNC presses and the very latest in computer aided design and manufacture processes are used in the service of their excellent product range. Caravans today are 'technocrafted', a far cry from those early days when Martin Bailey put together that first caravan entirely by hand.

Bailey take pride in the build quality and water resistance of their caravans. From each batch of new tourers, one is pulled out and put through a test that takes in its towing performance over a set course and its resistance to water leaks. Using recycled water, the caravan is tested for an entire day.

Right: *A Bailey CNC machine.*
Below: *Bailey caravans used in the BBC Driver of the Year competition in the 1970s.*

Another great selling point for Bailey tourers is the low depreciation and consequently high resale value of all models. In addition, a higher than average proportion of purchasers change for another Bailey, time after time.

The Senator range heads up the Bailey tourer line-up and all six models combine the latest in touring luxury and practicality. The stylish and practical interiors come with padded and jute-backed carpets, plus a choice of upholstery designs and materials with matching bolsters/scatter cushions and fully lined curtains. Also standard on these top specification tourers are 86-litre Electrolux fridges with full-width freezer compartments and electronic ignition, mains lighting and many other improvements including new fold-up worktops in the kitchen.

So that people in all other parts of the country get their chance to check out the superior specifications of a Bailey

caravan, the company runs a National Caravan Roadshow from the sites of all its dealers across the country. The 2001 line-up includes 19 models from the award winning Ranger, Pageant and Senator ranges, offering a layout, specification and price to suit all requirements

At the end of the production line, every tourer is put through a 50 point check to ensure it's in perfect working order. It's the 'belt and braces approach' to checks on every appliance in the caravan, from light switches to the hob and oven unit.

Of course nowadays there are many people on the Bailey staff, each offering an area of expertise to the company, whether technical, assembly, sales or administration. The calibre of the staff is one of the main reasons that the company is in the position it is today.

The company continues to be forward looking and is presently developing a new factory in Bristol, demonstrating their confidence in the product and their commitment to modern design and production facilities. This will all help the firm to keep and perhaps even improve its market share. All this is good news for the owners of Bailey caravans, who can look forward to many more years of service, Bailey-style as well as the development of products which will continue to push at the boundaries of mobile home comfort and technical excellence. The firm is interested in the motorhome market and it is possible that it will be making it own high quality contribution to this growing industry. Bailey is understandably reluctant to speculate too much on the future intentions. But some things remain certain. There will be no departure from the 'tried and tested' approach which has stood the company in such good stead throughout its history to date. Such is the company's success in driving production and material costs down that a departure from traditional procedures may not be wise. Only the innermost circle of management at Bailey know what's in store for the future but everyone can be sure that there are many more years in the Bailey story still to be written.

Above: *A Bailey 'Corsair' from the early 1980s.* ***Above left:*** *Leo Beckett and The RT. Hon Margaret Beckett MP, Secretary of State for the environment, food and rural affairs, and Patrick Howard, Chairman of Bailey Caravans on Mr and Mrs Beckett's tour of the factory.* ***Below:*** *An aerial view of the Bailey Caravan site, 2001.*

On the home front

A mug of strong, hot tea, a sandwich, a few minutes' rest - and a smile and a word of encouragement from the girls staffing the mobile canteen - it was just what this band of tired soldiers needed. Which of Bristol's bomb sites had they been working to clear, we wonder? Soldiers, Civil Defence workers, fire services - all of them did marvellous work when Hitler's bombs began to rain down on the city. Putting their own lives on the line to rescue people trapped in the ruins of their own homes, and sometimes performing the gruesome task of retrieving the bodies of those who didn't make it, these weary men surely deserved champagne and caviar! Mobile canteens, usually staffed by members of the Women's Voluntary Service (Her Majesty the Queen paid tribute to the work of the WVS in 1966 by adding 'Royal' to the title), performed a vital service during the war years. Many of the canteens were donated by charitable organisations, and as we can see, this one was a gift from the American Red Cross. Established in all civilised nations under the 1864 Geneva Convention, the Red Cross societies were from the beginning dedicated to the care of the wounded in wartime.

Any old iron? 'Dig out that junk!' This enthusiastic garage owner in Southville set up his own wartime appeal for 'metal for munitions'. Iron, brass or lead, all was grist to his mill, and displaying some of the donations of tin kettles, battered saucepans and even an old bike in his front garden paid off. He was able to raise £1.10s in his first week for the benefit of the Red Cross organisation.

When the government asked the people of Britain to donate their iron and scrap for the war effort, there was an overwhelming response from those who wanted to see their old bikes and railings turned into Spitfires and Hurricanes. Door to door collections produced a creditable pile of scrap metal, and a catchy little verse helped things along: 'The war is driving Hitler back, But here's one way to win it. Just give your salvage men the sack And see there's plenty in it'. It was all a morale boosting exercise; the people who gave items they could ill afford to part with had no way of knowing that their sacrifice was largely in vain. Sadly, little of the scrap metal collected during the campaign ever left the scrap yards.

Devastation came to Union Street during December 1940, and little remains of Smarts store, near the top of the hill. Still bravely clinging to the wall are the sign boards bearing its name, and a few supporting walls. Inside, the floors, walls, ceilings, and staircases, the counters, shelves and the entire stock, are gone. Blackened beams hang in space, supporting nothing. A couple of ladies, shocked and saddened at the sight, chat with a man whom we take to be an ARP warden. None of them appears to be concerned about the precarious state of the masonry above them, but this was, after all, wartime, and people were quite used to picking their way to and from work through piles of bricks and debris.

It was as far back as 1935 that the establishment of a Home Office ARP Department was approved, and the ARP act was passed in December 1937. Air Raid Wardens were responsible for the safety of the general public, along with other organisations such as fire fighters, medical services, messengers, nurses, ambulance drivers and others - and they did far more for Bristol than shout 'Put that light out!' during the blackout! They worked tirelessly and selflessly during air raids, dealing with incendiary bombs with their trusty stirrup pumps, and rescuing trapped victims from the wreckage of their burning homes.

Above: Not perfect by any means, but a coat of shatter-proof laquer was less unsightly than rows of brown tape criss-crossing your windows. This was June 1940, and during the war the danger of flying glass was very real; a bomb exploding even some distance away would shatter your own windows. As early as 1938 the Home Office had prepared a booklet entitled 'The Protection of your Home against Air Raids', which was sent to every home in Britain. The booklet suggested that 'if this country were ever at war', people should cover their windows with a couple of thin sheets of translucent, non-inflammable material, using cellulose varnish as an adhesive. A year later, it was all a ghastly reality, and preparations had to be made for those air raids. Whatever was your preferred method of protecting your windows, your vision and light were reduced. But after all, 'there was a war on', as people often repeated to each other, and you did what you had to do. Other preparations for defence were made across the country, and thousands of sandbags were filled and used to protect public buildings, shops, pubs, and churches. Well-loved and precious statues such as Eros in Piccadilly Circus were removed to places of safety, and precious works of art were taken into hiding.

Both pictures: Another casualty of war (above). The night of 2nd December 1940 saw Bristol's second 'blitz', and this double deck bus, pictured on Burlington Road corner in Whiteladies Road, was badly hit during the raid. Boys, so they say, will be boys, and several were drawn to 'ooh and ah' over the damage. Death and destruction had rained down on the city from 6.15 in the evening to 4.00 in the morning - it must have seemed never ending to those sitting in cellars, below the stairs, and in air raid shelters, wondering whether

they would be the next victims. A total of 121 German planes droned overhead, their incendiaries falling to set fire to buildings, their high explosive bombs plummeting down to blast houses, roads, shops and warehouses apart. More than 1,500 firemen fought the fires, and two Auxiliary Fire Service men were among the 156 people killed that night. The bus pictured here was taken out of service for a time; spare parts were as rare as hens' teeth, but it eventually had a refit and returned to the streets of Bristol complete with a new body. Repair and maintenance of the fleet was a real dilemma during the war. Petrol was strictly rationed, and in 1940 it rose in price to 1/11d a gallon. At a time when more people than ever were using public transport, many buses were falling victim to bombing raids and were unusable.

As the men of Bristol left to join the services, women stepped in to fill the gaps, training for jobs they had never done before. Some became bus conductresses, and the cheerful 'clippies' became a familiar sight on the city's buses (top). Some went on to become drivers, and the girls pictured here were the original seven who took the course. Three of them passed the driving test - in fact Mrs Violet Hoyes, third from the left in the photograph, made history as Bristol's very first female bus driver. Lovers of detail will perhaps like to know that Mrs Hoyes' bus was a Bedford single decker. The blackout caused a lot of headaches for drivers, who not only had to 'feel' their way around the city streets, but needed to know their routes like their own backyards. Inside the vehicles, the lights were so dim that the unfortunate conductresses scarcely knew whether they were being given a halfpenny or a shilling!

Above: These sandbags are well past their sell-by date, but never mind - they make great playthings for every passing youngster to stick their fingers into. And when did dirt and old sand down the fingernails ever bother your average five-year-old? This charming photograph was taken on 21st September 1939. The local streets were the playground for these kiddies, as they were for many of us, but back then parents could allow their children to play out without the kind of worries which keep today's children imprisoned indoors or in their gardens. The streets were where we played tin can squat, chased our hoops, and whipped our tops; the alleyways the place we played hide and seek and endless games of cowboys and Indians, wielding our unmenacing toy guns (armed, if we had a penny to spare, with percussion caps). Life was much simpler - and safer - back then, and though today's children have their own TV sets, computers with the accompanying expensive games, and countless toys, one can't help but think that that wonderful ingredient of childhood - freedom - has been stolen from them. Our photograph reveals a further difference - a noticeable lack of litter on the street. A fact which speaks for itself and needs no further comment...

Below: 'She's the girl that makes the thing that drills the hole that holds the spring that drives the rod that turns the knob that works the thingamabob....' So went the popular wartime song. What a pity we can't see just what these female workers were doing! Their place of work, like so many during the blitz, had been bombed - but that spirit of 'true grit' that prevailed during the war, they refused to be beaten, and setting up work tables and benches outside they moved their entire operation out into the street. When Britain's men were called into military service, women found themselves doing jobs they had never done before. Many of them worked in machine shops and engineering factories, turning out armaments and aeroplane parts, work that had always been looked on as 'jobs for the men'. Women did a good job - and what is more, they found themselves enjoying the work. The degree of independence that a weekly wage gave them was to raise a few problems after the war, when many of them didn't want to give up their jobs and go back to their old lives.

This photograph raises more questions than it answers, prompting us to wonder what was on the other end of the long rope these boys are pulling on with so much enthusiasm. It is doubtful, however, that we will ever find out - unless, of course, one of our readers recognises himself wearing short trousers in this fascinating photograph! The four small boys pictured here in the ruins of St Francis' Church are doing what small boys have always enjoyed doing - messing about, exploring, experimenting, and getting dirty. The date was April 1941, and these smartly uniformed lads were probably members of a church-based organisation. The young members of organisations such as the Boys' Brigade, the Boy Scouts and the Messenger Service played a vital part in the war, often showing real bravery and selflessness. They may have been too young to fight - but they were all prepared to do their bit for Britain. St Francis', in North Street, Ashton, was rebuilt after the war - and interestingly, the theatre organ from the Gaumont Cinema was installed in the new church. Makes you wonder whether the worshippers ever joked about the organist appearing from the bowels of the building playing 'Zip-a-dee-doo-dah', doesn't it?

On the move

Men and women in hats and suits, long dark coats, and heavy dresses. Was this photograph, then, taken on a chilly February day? Not a bit of it. This was Bristol Bridge on 13th July 1938. If these people could only see us now, what would they think of the short shorts, bare legs, naked midriffs and pierced navels on show in our 21st century summers? How scandalised they would be! But this was the way we dressed back then, and no-one thought it at all strange to wear hats and coats on a warm summer's day. Other changes have come about since this image was caught by the camera. Britain was just a year away from war with Germany, declared on 3rd September 1939, and Nazi bombing raids would subsequently destroy the buildings to the left and right of this view. Tramcar No 19, here advising us to eat Harris's sausages, would, with the rest of the fleet, have given place to the motor bus and disappeared from our streets by 1941; and what about the prominent advertisement on the right? The sweeping claim that 'Germolene heals all skin trouble' is one which would doubtless be questioned today!

Above: It's March 1938, and the winter is only just past, but even so the crisp, bright sunshine has tempted a couple of passengers on to the top deck of this Bristol tram. It's a long time since we had open top trams in the city, and marvellous old photographs such as this tend to give us that 'good old days' feeling. But those who are old enough to remember them will recall how chilly those picturesque old trams could be! And the drivers were even worse off than the passengers. They were provided with leather aprons as protection from the weather, but we can imagine what a comfortless job tram driving would have been in a harsh winter. In the year of the photograph motor buses began to take over as the old trams were phased out. But when war broke out trams were kept in service until a bomb severed the power cables in 1941, leaving only two workable routes. It was the end of the line for Bristol's trams. Note the interesting direction signs at the road junction, which give far more precise distances than similar signs today: 'Avonmouth six and three quarters; Weston Super Mare 20 and a quarter.

Below: This was 'White Van Man' as he used to be before acquiring a supposed reputation as an unpopular, loud mouthed, rude-gesturing cutter-up of other drivers! Smart in his uniform, this White Van Man is obviously proud to work for Samuel Shield's Dyers and Cleaners in Colston Avenue, and with a parcel of freshly cleaned clothing in his hand, he and his Bedford van are ready for a new delivery run. Who could imagine him being anything other than polite and respectful to every other road user, from coal lorry driver to push bike rider? This photograph dates from 17th March 1936, and sixty years after Alexander Graham Bell invented the telephone, the phone number printed on the firm's van, 'Number 3 Filton', would appear a little inadequate; after all, we are told that by 1932 there were almost 30 million telephones around the world! But we suppose that the Filton numbers had to start somewhere.... Today we might look for those 'Three for the price of two' offers; but back then gentlemen could at least seize the opportunity to have their suits cleaned for half a crown at Samuel Shields' dry cleaning establishment . With average wages around £2.10s a week, not as cheap as it might at first appear.

Below: One-horse-power replaces the internal combustion engine in this wartime image, reminding us that petrol was precious and strictly rationed at the time. 'Give us the tools - we will finish the job,' reads the notice in the rear window, repeating the words of Winston Churchill to President Roosevelt in a radio broadcast in February that same year. This was 'War Weapons Week', held in July 1941 to encourage people to put their money into National Savings. During the second world war 'Weeks' were often held to raise funds, and the public were asked to contribute to one worthy cause or another: War Weapons Week in 1941, Warships in 1942, Wings for Victory in 1943 and Save the Soldier in 1944. These special events raised thousands of pounds for the war effort, but more importantly people felt that they were doing their part, however small, in winning the war. The war effort prompted much rivalry between local companies; the larger ones might raise £20,000 for a Wellington Bomber (to be repaid after the war), while small firms might manage to get a couple of thousand pounds together to pay for an aeroplane wing. Many towns and cities actually 'bought' Spitfires for £5,000, encouraged by the list of contributors to the war effort which was read out over the wireless every evening after the news.

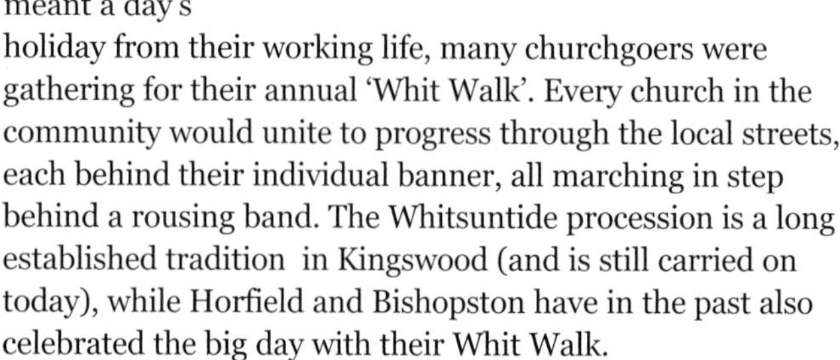

Above: The tramways centre, and though the days of the Bristol trams are numbered, the Clifton tramlines shine in the hazy February sunshine. This is 1939, and though the outbreak of war is still several months away, changes are already underway in the Centre. In the background, construction work goes on as a stretch of the River Frome, which had been a busy quay since the 13th century, is covered in. Today the Frome still flows, though unseen. The pleasant flower beds which once bloomed here, however, are gone, and have been replaced by our controversial water feature. To the left of the photograph is Colston Tower, where we can today relax with our friends over a glass or two at Yates' Wine Lodge. To the right stands the BTCC office and canteen; closed down in the 1980s, a modern office block was built on the site. The tramway clock is a well known landmark; remember the two others which existed, one at the Old Market and the other at Lawrence Hill depot? Note the long pedestrian crossing, marked out by the studs and yellow beacons which were introduced in 1934 by the Minister of Transport, Leslie Hore Belisha. Across Britain, the crossings were given their zebra stripes in 1951.

Top right: A holiday feeling is in the air as long queues form at the bus stands in Colston Avenue. It's Whit Monday 1955 - 30th May - and while the girls in their teens and 20s are out in their flowered summer dresses, the older ladies are playing safe and sticking with their more sensible coats. A day's outing to Clevedon or Weston-Super-Mare, or perhaps to Bath, was a popular choice on the rare bank holidays when office workers could cover their typewriters and shop assistants hang up their overalls and let their hair down. Whitsuntide was a key date in the church calendar in those far-off days before the advent of today's secular 'spring bank holiday'. Churches often held special Whit Sunday services to mark Pentecost, and while for large numbers of people Whit Monday simply meant a day's holiday from their working life, many churchgoers were gathering for their annual 'Whit Walk'. Every church in the community would unite to progress through the local streets, each behind their individual banner, all marching in step behind a rousing band. The Whitsuntide procession is a long established tradition in Kingswood (and is still carried on today), while Horfield and Bishopston have in the past also celebrated the big day with their Whit Walk.

Bottom right: A familiar sight to many of our readers who huddled, damp and chilled to the bone, beneath them at the end of many a working day - the draughty old bus shelters which used to stand in the Centre. The shelters were, of course, eventually removed, and in an interesting and perhaps praiseworthy move towards recycling, they were not destroyed but taken away and re-erected in the city's suburbs, where they were used until quite recently.

Though the businesses occupying these premises in Colston Avenue may have changed, the buildings themselves survived to the present day. Not so the road system, however. At the time of the photograph, traffic circuited the Centre in a counter clockwise direction. A few years on would see the direction reversed.

Greater changes were about to take place, as the Centre became choked with traffic that threatened to bring the city to a standstill, especially during the daily rush hour. The end of the 20th century was to see large scale roadworks and the introduction of the dramatic and controversial new traffic system which would propel many of Bristol's drivers protesting into the new millennium.

Cars parked in the bus stands in Colston Street? This strange scene, caught on camera on 23rd July 1957, is one which was echoed in many towns and cities across Britain back in the 1950s, and its cause was a walkout by bus drivers and conductors. The strike made it difficult to find a parking place in the city, and these smart car owners who nabbed the bus stands were the lucky ones. If you owned a car in the 1950s you were fortunate indeed; other commuters had to brush off the dust and pump up the tyres of their old push bikes, while even more were reduced to 'shanks's pony'. However sympathetic the commuters were with the demands of the busmen, that did not solve their immediate problem, which was to get to and from work. The Thatcher Government of the 1980s introduced measures to curb trade unions' power to strike, and in 1984 an Act was passed that made a secret ballot of members obligatory before a strike.

Redevelopment took away the buildings on the right of the photograph, but those who drove our buses at the time will clearly remember the Maritas cafe, which opened early enough for them to pop in for a morning brew.

Below: If you were looking for a good second-hand car, then the RCA showroom, where Gus Collins was at the helm, was the place to go. 'Large showroom at rear - walk in and look around, no obligation to purchase,' a rather wordy sign in the windscreen of one of the cars tells passers-by. But once you were inside, you might well be tempted by a shiny black Ford, or even a Rover - and if you had a couple of hundred pounds in your pocket to leave as a deposit, you could drive one home the same day. By the early 1950s, ordinary families were beginning to experience the long promised post-war prosperity, and a car, once a far-off dream, was at last a possibility. The small and reliable Morris Minor, such as the car on the far left, selling for £795, was a popular choice; the Minor became the first all-British car to sell more than one million.

A poster on the pub wall informs us that the Kings Cinema, built by a workforce of demobbed men and opened in 1921, was showing 'The Magic Box', starring Robert Donat, at the time. A world away from its final film in 1976, 'The Sex Machine'! The Kings suffered an ignominious slide into soft porn and eventually made way for a modern office block.

Bottom: Bristol motorists must have often wondered why, in an expanding universe, they still could not find a parking place. Parking in the city, however, is not a 21st century problem; back in 1936 the Council published a leaflet entitled 'Where to Park Your Car in the Centre of Bristol'! This photograph of the Wine Street car park from High Street dates from July 1954, and as the city grew and new buildings were constructed, fewer and fewer open spaces such as this one - part of which was destined to be dedicated to the banking world - remained to the frustrated motorist. Wine Street lies to the left of the view, with the spire of St Paul's - now closed - on the skyline. More mature readers may remember lunching at the British Restaurant in the centre background for a mere 1/6d; wartime rationing led to the setting up of more than 2,000 subsidised 'British Restaurants' around the country, serving basic but wholesome food such as vegetables and stew followed by a steamed pudding and custard. The prices were deliberately kept low in an attempt to keep the nation healthy. To its right is the tower of St Peter's church, now a memorial to those Bristolians who died during World War II.

Shopping spree

The well-stocked windows of Strode Cosh & Penfold have enticed a couple of young ladies to stand and gaze, and hopefully choose and buy! The scene was captured in April 1957; the war had been over for a decade, all rationing had finally ended in July 1954, and the welcome days of plenty had arrived in Britain. The shopkeepers of the 50s, keen to show the world that the days of empty shelves and make do and mend were long gone, crammed their display windows to bursting point with goods for sale. As we can see, fashion too had been affected by the atmosphere of plenty; gone were the skimpy lines of utility clothing, and Dior's generous 'A-line', launched in 1955, is reflected in the clothing of these young women. Strode Cosh & Penfold's was, as readers may remember, much more than your average chemist's shop! Their building on the corner of Broadmead and Lower Union Street was only three years old at the time of the photograph, and was destined to stand for less than half a century. It was later to be demolished and replaced by the Tesco supermarket and Metro stores we know today.

The market in High Street was always a good starting place for the housewives of Bristol, who week after week would catch a bus into town and tour the market to find the best - and cheapest - fruit and vegetables. April 1938, when this picture was taken was not the most affluent of times for the ordinary person in the street. The lady with the open shopping basket pictured here with her husband would perhaps shop around and buy potatoes and cabbage from one stall, carrots and a swede from another and, if the housekeeping money would stretch to it, maybe a pound of apples and a few bananas from a third. The war years saw bananas disappear from our shops, not to reappear until 1946. Children born during the war had never seen a banana, and had no idea that they had to peel off the skin before they could eat the fruit. The Home Secretary actually went on the radio, giving children instructions how they should open and eat them!

St Nicholas' Market has changed little if at all since this scene was recorded, and perhaps the very same units are still in use today, embellished of course by modern green and orange scalloped awnings!

Above: As if we were not already aware of the nature of Carwardine's business, the window display of tea pots and coffee-making accessories says it all, and on a pleasant day in the late 1950s, the gaily striped awning shades the windows of one of Bristol's most well known coffee bars from the sunshine. A firm favourite with shoppers whose tired feet demanded a rest, Carwardine's was a popular place to meet friends, and three elderly ladies, in their smart suits and neat little hats - the badge of the 1950s - step out briskly towards the doorway, looking forward, no doubt, to their morning coffee and cakes. Remember that wonderful smell of freshly ground coffee that wafted across the pavement to tempt passers-by?

During the 1950s, coffee bars gained in popularity, overtaking the milk bars which used to be seen on every high street. Carwardine's coffee bar was on the corner of Horsefair and Lower Union Street. Earlier years had seen a watering hole of quite a different character in this position when the old Haymarket Tavern still stood, catering for Bristolians' thirst. The pleasant Victorian pub was lost to the city during the post-war redevelopment of Bristol. The shop premises across the road were to be given a facelift in the 1980s.

Though it is only 9.30 in the morning, this group of Bristol housewives look weary already. It was April 1964, and with domestic freezers still a luxury item which few could afford, the woman of the house still had to shop for fresh food several times a week. Cater, Stoffell & Fortt was a favourite port of call; our readers will perhaps remember the old traditional grocery store with a touch of nostalgia. From the ordinary housewife to the smart young woman in stiletto heels, whatever your palate demanded, this wonderful old grocer's could supply it. Even the little dog in the photograph - whose mistress obviously shopped here - looks well fed and happy! Bacon, sliced as you wanted it by one of those dangerous looking machines; cheese soft and hard, mild Cheddar or Blue Stilton; 'best' butter or Stork margarine; garlic sausage or slices of salami; and eggs large and small, each with a little lion stamped on it. 'Go to work on an egg,' the British Egg Marketing Board encouraged us from 1957 onwards, together with the slogan 'You can rely on the Lion'. The lion stamp (due for a comeback?) was removed from eggs at the end of 1968.

Making a living

Below: Jobs for the boys, jobs for the girls: segregation was the norm back in the 1920s, and these young ladies working in regimented rows with weighing scales and piles of tobacco are workers in WD and HO Wills' tobacco factory. Tobacco was first imported from Virginia in 1639, and became a major source of revenue in Bristol. By 1901, the factory already had a workforce of 3,000. Many of the workers were young women, and when they applied for employment the girls were given a sewing test to prove their deftness of hand. The workplace dictated their lifestyle both in and out of the factory; before they were given a job they had to produce references from their Sunday Schools, and were required to sign indentures agreeing that as long as they were employed by the company they would not become engaged to be married or gamble. Wills', however, cared about their workers, providing annual outings and, from 1891, annual paid holidays.

It was definitely a man's world at the time, and it was not until the country was in the grip of 1960s flower power that girls began to rebel. Burning their bras (emotionally if not actually), they formed the women's liberation movement and in a male dominated society dared to demand equal rights and opportunities for women.

Bottom: Drilling and filling were history as far as Mr Williams' dental chair was concerned, and Bristolians with tooth decay would suffer in it no more. The chair came in handy, however, as an impromptu 'advertisement board' after a severe air raid wiped out the dental surgery at 2, Dolphin Street in December 1940. Nothing daunted, Mr Williams moved, lock, stock and a few smoking drills and set up once more at Number 26 Bridge Street, opposite the old Scholastic. Unfortunately, it was not a good choice of address as just a few weeks later Bridge Street - including Number 26 - also fell victim to an enemy air raid, and Mr Williams was forced into another move. Was it a case of 'third time lucky' we wonder?
With all its grim realities, wartime nevertheless gave humorists the opportunity to boost morale with samples of their wit. 'More open for business than usual', for example, might appear outside a partly-bombed shop or pub, and the sight of this dentist's chair would have brought many a smile to the faces of passers by. Bristol's second 'blitz', on the night of 2nd December 1940, cost the lives of 156 people and injured 270 others.

BELG
FISHIN
BOAT
MACHINE-GUN
EVENING
WORL
NORWAY
AT WAR
IF-
EVENING
WORLD
SCAN
HITL
AN

A grim expression is on the face of this news vendor in the High Street (left), whose paper carries the latest news of Hitler's doings in Europe. It was 6th April 1940, seven months after Britain had declared war against Germany. After the initial scare, when air raid sirens had sounded immedately after the declaration, things had gone very quiet, and people began talking about the 'phoney war'. But these news headlines remind us that in Europe things were very different. Norway and Denmark lay geographically in the way of Hitler's plans, and on 9th April Germany invaded both countries. The possibility of his negotiating a peace with Britain and France was abandoned, and the phoney war was over. Before long the war would become a grim reality for the people of Bristol. The Angel Fountain, set into the wall of St Nicholas' Church, was later removed to a place of safety. St Nicholas' itself was one of the many places of worship that fell victim to enemy bombs.

During the war, every day brought important news. 'Holland and Belgium Invaded' the Bristol Evening Post placard shouted on 10th May 1940 (below), and even the news vendors stationed by the Angel Fountain have their heads deep in the newspaper, obviously worried about the implications of this particular item of news. It was Holland and Belgium's turn to hit the headlines; claiming that he believed that the British and French were making preparations to attack Germany through the Netherlands, Belgium and Luxembourg, Hitler had marched in to occupy the Low Countries, even though they had repeatedly declared their decision to remain neutral. Hitler claimed that he had 'irrefutable evidence' of Allied invasion plans. Belgium's protest that they had proof that Germany's offensive was premeditated fell, of course, on deaf ears. The 'phoney war' was over for the Low Countries and France. With the occupation of Belgium the Maginot Line was circuited and the door into France was wide open. The 4th June saw British troops hastily evacuated from Dunkirk back to Britain; by the 25th, fighting in France had ended.

The 10th May was a key date in the 1940 calendar, and other news in this same paper would report that Chamberlain had resigned and that Winston Churchill had taken over as Britain's new Prime Minister.

Above: Younger Bristolians would have trouble placing Philadelphia Street. Redevelopment has so transformed the area that no point of reference remains in this photograph which dates from February 1957, but Philadelphia Street was parallel with Merchant Street, which today runs alongside the Galleries shopping centre. The view captures an important piece of Bristol's almost forgotten history - the chapel in the background, which was George Whitfield's Tabernacle in Penn Street. During the 18th century, the established Church of England was largely out of touch with the working classes, and George Whitfield, an Anglican evangelist who had been a missionary in the American colonies, decided to do something about it. As a dissenter, the church doors of Bristol were barred against him, so he took the gospel to huge crowds, mainly of miners' families, in the open air. Between March and December of 1739 he and the famous John Wesley joined forces in bringing Christianity to the working people. Of Bristol's 20,000 population at the time, one fifth were dissenters.
By 1959, Whitfield's little Tabernacle had gone, another piece of history replaced by one of the new stores which sprang up around the city during its redevelopment.

Top right: With the Labour Exchange in Nelson Street to the left, where over the years thousands of luckless souls waited in dreary queues, the view - which has changed drastically over the last 30 years - looks from Myers' multi-storey car park towards Rupert Street. The year was 1964; building sites have been cleared, and within a few years construction work would begin on the Police Headquarters and the Magistrates' Court (with its 'passageway in the sky'). The old Bridewell police station can be seen in the right foreground - and spot the old police Road Traffic Department, almost dead centre. The 150ft Cabot Tower juts into the skyline on the far left of this shot. The tower was built to commemorate the historic voyage of John Cabot, who set sail with his son Sebastian in 1497 in the 'Matthew' in search of a western route to India, landing in Newfoundland. To the right of the tower, the twin gables of the former printing works which is now the University School of Drama; other university buildings dominate the skyline.

Far right: It was the end of the 1950s, and as we can see from the gigantic cranes which stand out against the sky, Bristol was in a fever of reconstruction when this view of Fairfax Street was captured in September 1959. Shoppers at Woolworths were oblivious to the work - they were used to it! Today, such features as the old castle wall and Fairfax House are long gone, and we can 'shop till we drop' at The Galleries shopping centre, where we can find virtually anything we need under one roof. Being able to browse under cover means a lot to shoppers running the gauntlet of the British climate. Older readers will spot the

old News Theatre in the process of demolition in the background; having almost miraculously survived the World War II bombing raids which destroyed nearby buildings, it was closed in April 1956 for road development. The News Theatre was very small in comparison with other cinemas, having only 385 seats. In the days before television hit Britain in a big way, newsreel film was popular with the punters - as were the cartoons. Newsreel cinemas were well known in London, but the Bristol News Theatre was the first of its kind outside the metropolis.

A bus to the skies

The headquarters of Airbus UK are located at Filton, Bristol which is also home to its main design and engineering facilities. The company's manufacturing activities are carried out at Filton and at Broughton in North Wales. Together these two sites employ around 10,000 people.

At the turn of the new century Airbus programmes were securing some 62,000 jobs in the UK in over 400 companies , including Rolls Royce Aero-engines which supplies power plants to an increasing number of Airbus models.

Airbus UK is the British arm of the Airbus company. BAE SYSTEMS owns 20 per cent of the company and European Aeronautic Defence and Space Company (EADS) 80 per cent. Fokker in the Netherlands and Belairbus in Belgium are also associated with some Airbus programmes. In June 2000 BAE SYSTEMS and EADS, then partners in the Airbus Industrie consortium, announced the formation of a new Airbus integrated company. The new company, known simply as 'Airbus', incorporating both Airbus Industrie and all the major Airbus activities of BAE SYSTEMS and EADS was formed on 11th July 2001.

The prime responsibility of Airbus UK is the design and manufacture of high-technology wings for all Airbus models as well as overall design and supply of fuel systems. For most Airbus models the company is also responsible for the design and manufacture of landing gear and, in the case of the Airbus A321, the design and manufacture of a section of the fuselage.

As world leaders in wing design and technology Airbus UK has an unrivalled engineering team; its expertise is enhanced by working with some of the world's leading aerospace research establishments.

Above: *Sir George White, Founder and Chairman of the British and Colonial Aeroplane Co Ltd.* ***Below:*** *The Bristol Exhibition Bus, 1920.*

Airbus UK engineers focus on innovative research and development. Advanced aerodynamic and structural designs, low cost production techniques and the use of 'new' materials result in cost effective high performance wings which contribute to lower fuel consumption and reduced emissions - all of which ensures lower operating costs throughout the life of an aircraft.

But what are the origins of this world-renowned aircraft firm and what are its connections to Bristol?

In February 1910 the British and Colonial Aeroplane Company was set up in two sheds in the village of Filton. Work still continues nearby but there is now also a vast complex of factory buildings, offices, laboratories, testbeds, an airfield and other facilities spread over hundreds of acres.

Sir George White was the man who began it all in 1910. He was a wealthy Bristol businessman as well as a practical visionary who had already exploited the possibilities of tramways and motor buses both in Bristol and elsewhere. White was quick to see the potential of the aeroplane, not merely as a sporting vehicle but also as a revolutionary form of military and civil transport.

Within a few months the Bristol Challenger Biplane, known more commonly as the Boxkite, was coming off a well organised production line in the Filton factory at the rate of two a week. At the 1910 Autumn manoeuvres on Salisbury Plain the Boxkite operated successfully in an aerial reconnaissance role. In November of that year the company landed its first export order: eight Boxkites for Russia. To cater for the growing number of aspiring pilots the company opened its own training establishments at Larkhill and Brooklands.

From 1914 onwards the development of the company followed a clearly discernible pattern. Periods of explosive expansion in wartime were succeeded by periods of difficult readjustment to the lesser, and less urgent, demands of peacetime.

The first Bristol aircraft to be ordered in quantity for service in the First World War was the Scout, a single seat biplane with a top speed of around 100 mph. The Scout did sterling work as a reconnaissance, training and communication aircraft, but it was not designed for offensive operations.

Zeppelin raids and the growing ascendancy of the more heavily armed German aircraft over the Western Front

Above left: *The old Filton House in 1927.* ***Below:*** *The Zodiac Biplane on show at the Olympia Aero Show in March 1910. Numerically the first aeroplane to carry the Bristol name, the Zodiac was built in France and another five machines were set to be built under licence at Filton. However the Zodiac pictured here refused to fly and the project was abandoned but some parts that were already made were incorporated into the first true Bristol plane - the Challenger Biplane.*

pointed to the need for a genuine fighter plane. Filton's answer was the two seater Bristol Fighter, amongst the most famous military aircraft ever produced. In total around 5,300 Fighters were built at various locations. At the time of the Armistice in 1918 the company payroll had risen to 3,000 compared with 200 in August 1914 and the original two modest sheds had become part of a factory with eight acres of floor space.

There now followed what was in many respects the most difficult decade in the company's history, renamed in 1920 the Bristol Aeroplane Company. Problems of readjustment and survival were intensified by the general world wide economic depression that followed the short-lived post war boom. The aircraft business was supplemented by the production of bus and coach bodies and later motor car bodies. Fortunately the Bristol Fighter was selected by the RAF in 1919 as its standard army co-operation machine. Construction of new Fighters and the reconditioning of existing ones to meet the RAF's requirements brought a steady flow of work to the Filton workshops.

__Top:__ The Bristol Challenger Biplane, 1910. This Biplane (works no. 7) bearing competition no. 19 was the first Filton designed and built aeroplane and the first Bristol machine to fly. It first flew on 30 July 1910. __Above:__ The Bristol Scout (Type C), August 1914.

In 1920, in the year that the British & Colonial Aeroplane Company Ltd went into voluntary liquidation and its assets transferred to its sister company the Bristol Aeroplane Company, the Cosmos Engineering Company, located in the Fishponds area of Bristol, was acquired. The small group of Cosmos engineers had earlier designed the Jupiter and Lucifer air-cooled radial aero-engines and these were developed to become the first of a long and distinguished line of Bristol engines.

In 1929 the Bristol Bulldog won a fiercely contested competition for adoption as the RAF's new single-seat day and night fighter. Manoeuvrability and maintainability were two qualities that endeared the Bulldog to pilots and ground crew alike. Nearly 450 Bulldogs were produced at Filton from 1929 to 1934 and a number of foreign forces followed the RAF's example in choosing the Bulldog for their airforces. In the 1920s and 30s Bristol was closely associated with attempts on the world altitude record. The record changed hands nine times in the ten years 1928-38 and on six of those occasions the aircraft were powered by Bristol engines. Twice, in 1936 and 1937, the special Bristol Type 138 high altitude monoplane captured the record for Britain. This was not the end of Bristol's success in this field: in 1953 and 1955 an Olympus powered English Electric Canberra piloted by WF Gibb set new altitude records.

In 1935 however the British Government launched a rearmament programme. Bristol like all the other major British aviation companies was encouraged to expand production and gear up for war.

In the six months from June to December the workforce grew from 4,200 to more than 8,200 as production of the Blenheim light bomber began. The Blenheim had its origins in a twin engined monoplane design, the Bristol Type 142. A prototype 142 had been ordered by Lord Rothermere as a private high speed transport and was named by him the 'Britain First'. In its airworthiness acceptance trails the 142 demonstrated a top speed of 285 mph, 50 mph faster than any fighter then in service.

Two figures give a measure of the massive contribution made by Bristol to the national war effort, either directly or through 'shadow factories'. In all, more than 14,000 Bristol aircraft and over 100,000 Bristol engines were manufactured.

The importance of Bristol's contribution was fully recognised by the enemy. In a daylight raid on the factories in September 1940 91 people were killed and more than 100 injured. This hastened the dispersal moves already underway and by 1942 with a payroll of 52,000, over 100 dispersal premises were in use.

The three aircraft types which accounted for the great bulk of Bristol's wartime production were the Blenheim, the Beaufighter and the Beaufort.

After the war the company again found itself having to cope with the problem of peacetime retrenchment and readjustment. Those problems had been foreseen and plans had been laid to meet them. As after the Great War a policy of diversification was now adopted and the company turned part of its design and production capacity to such varied projects as cars, factory built houses (using aluminium supplies from the breaking up of wartime aircraft) and plastic products.

A helicopter department was set up and this later became a large self-contained division at Weston-Super-Mare where the Sycamore and Belvedere helicopters were manufactured.

An immediate civil aircraft project was to hand in the Bristol Freighter, and its passenger version, the Wayfarer. More than 200 were built and served in

Top left: *The Bristol F2B Fighter Mk IV Type 96A, fitted with a Falcon Engine and with dual controls, circa mid 1920s.* ***Left:*** *The Bristol Bulldog Type 105 Mk II single seat fighter, circa 1930.*

all parts of the world. Far more ambitious was the Brabazon: in 1945 the company was awarded a prototype contract.

Although for economic and technical reasons the eight-engined Brabazon was never used in passenger service the project was a sound investment for Britain. Basic knowledge gained in the design and construction of this first big British airliner was invaluable, not only to Bristol but also to the entire British aviation industry.

Bristol applied the basic knowledge learned through the Brabazon to good effect in the turboprop Britannia. This was the first turbine powered airliner to provide a non-stop service over the North Atlantic. BOAC (British Overseas Airways Corporation) began Britannia services in 1957 and for nearly ten years thereafter Britannia airliners continued to operate in front line airline service.

A post war development of great significance was the company's entry into the field of guided missiles. After extensive research, involving rocket range testing in the UK and Australia the Bloodhound surface to air guided weapon system was adopted by the RAF and became a major export success. Bristol's' Guided Weapons team had to design and produce much of the advanced electronic test instrumentation required in the course of developing the Bloodhound. The highly specialised skills acquired in this work were later exploited in a variety of successful commercial applications not least when guided weapons production at Filton eventually ceased in 1989.

Even more significant was the company's work in the development of supersonic transport aircraft. Since the late 1950s Bristol played a principal role in the evolution of supersonic airliner proposals and would eventually become the British design and production centre for the Anglo/French Concorde.

Top: *An aerial view of the Filton works in 1939, shortly after being camouflaged.* ***Above right:*** *The Bristol Brabazon (Type 167) flying over the Gloucestershire countryside in November 1949.*

In the 50 years up to the formation of the British Aircraft Corporation in 1960 the Bristol company had produced over 15,000 aircraft of 85 different designs and in addition some 8,000 Bristol aircraft were built under licence in other countries.

The British Aircraft Corporation was formed on 1st July 1960 by the merging of the interests of English Electric, Vickers and the Bristol Aeroplane Company in the ratios 40:40:20 - with Bristol as the poor relation. The merger was a direct result of pressure from the Tory government which was based on the need to reduce defence expenditure and its plans to reshape defence policy around nuclear weapons and rockets rather than manned aircraft. Little work came to Filton and without new work the Filton site was in serious danger of closure. It was only saved by the transfer of work on the Lightning mk IV, Canberra, Valiant and VC10, until Concorde arrived with the massive amount of work which that famous aircraft would involve.

British involvement in Airbus dates back to the mid 1960s when design concepts were first exchanged with major European aircraft manufacturers. In 1967 the British, French and German governments signed a 'Tripartite Memorandum of Understanding' which initiated the Airbus A300 aeroplane as a project study. On May 28th 1969 the Airbus programme was launched by the French and German governments with one of Airbus UK's predecessor companies - Hawker Siddeley Aviation - participating in a sub-contract role with responsibility for the design and manufacture of wings.

The establishment of Airbus Industrie as a consortium in December 1970 by the French and Germans was the first step towards the integration of the European civil aviation industry. Since then Airbus has steadily gained market share and would become one of only two manufacturers in the world offering commercial airliners seating more than 100 passengers.

That prosperous future was not initially helped much by the British government which in December 1970 announced that it would not back the Airbus project financially, despite Hawker Siddeley having obtained contracts to provide wing design and subsequent production.

In March 1977 British Aerospace was established by the Aircraft and Shipbuilding Industries act, with the shares of the predecessor companies British Aircraft

Above: *The Bristol Type 142M Blenheim Mk I, circa 1938.*
Below: *The Bristol type 175 Britannia 310 airliner, 1957. G-AOVB was the first of 18 series 312 Britannias sold to BOAC and was a long range version suitable for trans-Atlantic flights.*

Corporation (Holdings) Ltd, Hawker Siddeley Aviation Ltd, Hawker Siddeley Dynamics Ltd
and Scottish Aviation Ltd vested in the new corporation.

In January 1979 British Aerospace became a full decision-making partner in the Airbus consortium taking a 20 per cent share of Airbus leaving France and Germany with 37.9 per cent each and Spain holding the remainder. For each and every Airbus model British Aerospace (and subsequently Airbus UK) would invest huge sums in their launch and ongoing development costs.

To the surprise of those pundits who never like to see a success Airbus began to get orders. By 1979 British Aerospace had delivered its 100th set of Airbus wings, in 1988 the Queen's Award for Technological Achievement was presented to British Aerospace Filton for the design and development of the Airbus A320 wing and by 1989 460 orders were received in that year alone. The British government was impressed and agreed to make a large investment in the enterprise.

Repayment of capital and interest on that British government loan of £250 million for the A320 announced in 1984 would be completed in 1997 with the investment yielding £2 for every £1 loaned. A similar loan of £450 million made in 1987, to develop wings for the A330 and A340 was expected to yield to the UK Treasury £3 for each pound invested. In March 2000 the government agreed to lend another £530 million for investment in the A380.

Long before then however, in 1984, the Airbus management centre in the United Kingdom was moved to Filton controlling the work of ten British Aerospace factories involved in Airbus projects in the UK. The following year work started at Filton in a new £6 million Airbus A320 Wing Equipping Centre which would be opened by Princess Anne the following year. British Aerospace PLC was reorganised into separate subsidiary companies in January 1989 with Airbus activity now coming within the sphere of British Aerospace (Commercial Aircraft) Ltd which in turn set up three operating divisions, one of which would be the Airbus Division.

1989 also saw the official opening by Prime Minister Margaret Thatcher of the new £12 million British Aerospace Commercial Aircraft Airbus Division Technical Centre at Filton.

Confidence in the future was well placed. In July 1991 the Lord Mayor of Bristol visited Filton to see the 250th Airbus A320 wing set being despatched to Toulouse.

Three new companies were formed in 1992 to replace those which made up British Aerospace Commercial Aircraft. One of the new companies would be British Aerospace Airbus Ltd, a vital component of what would become in due course Airbus UK.

Since its birth Airbus has been leading the way with many airliner firsts; in 1974 the Airbus A300 became the first twin-aisle twin-engined airliner. The Airbus A320 was the first to use

Top right: *Loading a Bristol 403 car into a Silver City Freighter Type 170 mk 32, en-route to Bordeux, France from Bristol, 1954.* ***Top left:*** *Bristol Helicopters, the Type 171 Sycamore (left) and Type 192 Belvedere in flight, circa 1960.* ***Right:*** *Concorde final assembly at Filton pictured in March 1976.*

full fly-by-wire control and the A330 and A340 were the world's first and only airliners to be launched as a genuine, complementary combined programme. Airbus would also be the first company to launch a twin-aisle genuine twin-deck passenger aircraft - the Airbus A380.

By the opening of the 21st century more than 2,500 Airbus aircraft had been delivered to 187 operators world wide, delivering over 300 in the year 2000 alone and with orders stretching several years into the future, not least for the newly launched 555 seat double-decker Airbus A380 which sets a completely new standard of air travel.

Launched in December 2000, the Airbus A380 is the most advanced, spacious and efficient airliner ever conceived. The A380 embodies the most advanced technologies providing 15 to 20 per cent lower operating costs than any other large aircraft in the same class, up to 15 per cent longer range as well as lower fuel burn, less noise and lower emissions. With almost 50 per cent more floor space and only 35 per cent more seating the Airbus A380 ensures that all passengers have wider seats and aisles, open spaces in which to stretch their legs and access to lower deck amenities. Thanks to the A380's lower seat-mile costs airlines will be able to offer a much improved service at even lower prices.

Whilst offering all the advantages of a completely new design the Airbus A380 will extend the unique benefits of the Airbus family commonality into the very large aircraft sector. Thanks to the same cockpit layout, procedures and handling characteristics through fly by wire pilots will be able to make the transition to the A380 from other Airbus aircraft with minimal additional training.

Meanwhile progress continues towards the launch of the Airbus A400M, the world's most efficient military transport aircraft, uniquely combining the latest military and commercial aircraft technologies and designed to meet the needs of armed forces for the next 30 years.

Times have certainly changed since Sir George White began producing the Bristol Boxkite biplane back in 1910. But what a remarkable legacy we have been left by the countless thousands who have worked at Filton!

Top left: *An aerial view of the Filton works, July 2000.* ***Above left:*** *The A400M - The wings designed and built by Airbus UK at Filton will be the first to be made primarily from composite materials.* ***Below left:*** *The Airbus A380.* ***Below right:*** *The landing gear of the newest Airbus A340-600 which flew for the first time in April 2001.*

Virtute et Integrity

The enterprise and trading culture of Bristol must have agreed with Wilfred Thomas Burden. It was from offices at Queens Square in pre-war Bristol that he initially established the south western operation of a small company specialising in the supply and distribution of civil engineering materials. Today, having adopted its founders initials and with its headquarters in Bristol, that company has grown to be one of the leading businesses in the UK construction industry. In this brief overview we can trace some of the steps in the development of the WTB Group since its formation 70 years ago.

Occupying the sometimes delicate ground between suppliers and customers, Wilfred's watchword was integrity. He set his company's telephone number under the old telephone 'letter dialling' system as I.N.T.E.G.R.I.T.Y. The telex address was the same and Integrity was a quality that WT Burden brought to all his dealings.

The original business of WT Burden, commonly referred to as Burdens, grew quite rapidly in the 1930s and by the outbreak of the Second World War it had established a yard in Birmingham and offices in London and Bristol. Throughout the war years the company still managed to flourish. The south western arm subsequently moved from its offices in Queens Square, Bristol, to a stocking branch in Brislington (now the site of a McDonalds).

Above left: *Company founder, Mr WT Burden.*
Right and below: *Laying pipes in the 1940s.*

The south western half of the business remained at Brislington under the guidance of Managing Director Mr. Martin Burton until 1955 when it moved to Culvers Road, Keynsham. It then remained there as a trading location and administration base until 1998.

Mr Burton remained as Managing Director and then Vice-Chairman of Burdens Western Ltd., (as the southern half of the company was known), until he died in 1987.

Mr WT Burden remained as Chairman of both halves of the company until his death in 1984. He was succeeded as Chairman by his son, Arthur, a Chartered Accountant who had only recently become involved with the business and who remains Chairman to this day. Arthur is also trustee of the Burdens Charitable Foundation which he helped his father establish with much of his father's shareholding.

Whilst the Burdens family and the Charitable Foundation still control the company, Arthur was instrumental in creating far wider share ownership within the management and employee base of the company. This has lead to the establishment of one of the country's first Inland Revenue approved Employee Share Schemes under which more than half the group's current employees now hold a stake and which has played a major part in recent growth.

Arthur oversaw the merging of the two halves of the business into one during the late 1970s with management re-centralised in Bristol under Alan Hampton as Managing Director. Under Alan and Arthur's guidance the company survived the worst ravages of the late seventies and early nineties recessions, and the scene was set for dramatic further expansion.

Now the current Chief Executive, Alan Hampton joined the firm from school and brings a thorough knowledge and commitment to the WTB enterprise, qualities which the company seeks to foster in all its employees.

Being enterprising enough to stock and distribute new products has always been a hallmark of the company and has contributed greatly to its success. Alan, as a key figure

Top: *A line-up of early company vehicles.*
Above: *Works outing circa 1954.*

in the business for over 35 years, has been chiefly responsible for this strategy.

The company were the first to stock clay drainage pipes with flexible mechanical joints introduced just after the second world war. This innovative approach laid the foundations for the company to become the largest supplier of drainage products in the UK.

The '90s could best be described as an expansive phase for the Group. It has made large investments in people, physical infrastructure, transport and IT systems. The WTB Group now has a National Distribution network with some 50 branches, and is in the top tier of its business class with a turnover approaching £200m. From the original six people employed by WT Burden the Group now employs some seven hundred.

The term 'Specialists' has been appropriately applied to differentiate the Group within its industry sector for many years and nowhere is this more evident than in the Group distribution function. Deliveries of half a million tonnes of materials per annum are carried out by well over 100 high specification crane off load delivery vehicles. A mobile phone in the cab of all the vehicles ensures excellent communication. An annual fuel spend of approx. £1million and in excess of £1/4 million on road fund licences is necessary to keep the fleet travelling in the order of 5 million miles a year or some 250 times around the world! WTB Group maintains "O" (Operators) licences in all eight licensing authority areas in England, Scotland and Wales.

Right: *Planting a commemorative tree at the opening of the Culvers Road, Keynsham branch - circa 1963.*
Below: *Loading materials in 1958.*

Customer care and product knowledge are key elements of the WTB distribution team. The 'heavy and dirty' nature of many of the products that the Group handle should not be overlooked and the 'specialist' skills and responsibilities of those drivers and distribution staff who undertake this work are a credit to the Group.

The close association with Bristol has strengthened over the years and in 1998 the Group head office was moved to Durley Park, Keynsham, an old National Grid Emergency Centre just off Durley Hill. Today Durley Park has been totally refurbished and provides high specification accommodation for the central staff supplying administration and support services to Group branches and businesses all over the UK.

In line with the Group's core commitment to quality and safety, all Burdens branches are accredited with the prestigious BS EN ISO 9002 accreditation, and all the specialist fleet are fitted with the most advanced safety equipment available.

The core commitments to quality and integrity are also evident in supplier and customer relationships, some of which go back over fifty years. The company's core expertise in drainage and civil engineering products gives it an innovative edge, which can be invaluable to suppliers and customers alike.

In keeping with the company's innovative and expansive view to business, the core quality product range of clay, concrete, plastic and iron drainage products has been widened and now includes; construction chemicals, street furniture, exterior lighting and signage, ducting systems, geotechnical and pressure pipeline products. The Group is also increasingly involved in the provision of specialist logistical services - principally to the de-regulating utility and multi-utility markets as they increasingly out-source distribution.

The ever present search for quality dictates that Burdens give these products their own back office 'technical

This page: *Work in the 1960s at the Lodge Hill Crematorium. WT Burden supplied special bricks to extend the chimney which can be seen in the picture below.*

support', and whilst these products can be something of a mystery to people on the street, without them comfortable urban life as we know it would not exist.

Apart from the everyday uses of these products by Local Authorities, Civil Engineering Contractors, Construction Companies, Utilities, Specialist Sub-Contractors and the like, the Company has also been privileged to supply materials to many high profile, and complex projects.

The company supplied geotextile products used to reclaim land for the Millennium Dome project, and then supplied specialist materials during the construction phases. The company supplied specialist materials on tight overnight delivery schedules to the Channel Tunnel and Second Severn Bridge and more recently has been involved in material supply to the Eden Project.

The company's ability to customise solutions and trading styles has been recognised by many high profile organisations. The Group's existing customer base includes national and regional civil engineering and construction companies, specialist sub-contractors, public and private utilities, local authorities and builders merchants.

Adopting an innovative approach to the physical stock and distribution of materials and the commercial administration associated with it's operations, the Group have been pioneers in supporting the development of a pan-European on line construction hub. The aim of this is to assist construction industry participants in reducing the costs involved with procurement of materials and sub-contracted works and the overall management of construction projects, offering clear opportunities to improve the efficiency of the construction industry supply chain.

Benefiting from a number of partnership arrangements with public utilities, and local authorities, and major contractors, Wilfred's watchword of I.N.T.E.G.R.I.T.Y continues to bear fruit today as the WTB Group supports the UK civil engineering industry.

Having grown from a small office and yard to being a Bristol based national company, the WTB Group expansion program is far from over. There are always opportunities to develop other branches, either on brown ground, or from greenfield sites. Equally the company is prepared to invest by company acquisition. In keeping with Bristol's history as an 'exploration' port, they have set sail and opened branches in Belfast and via acquisition have a significant presence in Dublin, owning the 'specialist' pipeline company Pipes Valves and Fittings.

As the world continues to become an ever smaller place the WTB Group are both importing and exporting materials

Top: *WT Burdens Western Ltd, at Keynsham circa 1970s.* ***Above:*** *Staff at WT Burdens Nottingham Branch pictured in 2001.*

around the globe. However the scale of the business has not detracted from the historical values and today the core values that Wilfred Thomas Burden laid down are still alive in the business and encompassed in the Group Vision:

- *To be the leading specialist distributor of civil engineering and construction materials*
- *Provide their trading partners with innovative supply chain solutions*
- *To build an environment in which everyone achieves their full potential*

Indeed the drive for excellence is evident throughout the organisation and covers the full extent of its activities from major employer to major supplier of drainage products to the construction industry.

Burdens Charitable Foundation

Mr and Mrs WT Burden would be very proud of the commercial success that has underpinned the work of the Foundation that they created. Over the past 20 years some 800 charities have benefited from the £2.4 million that the Foundation has donated. Another aim of the company is to achieve a reputation for being responsibly concerned for the well being of the local community in the area in which the company has a presence. A highlight in this area of the company's activity came in 1997 when £30,000 was raised through sponsorship for the Three Peaks Walk - the company's Charitable Foundation, the major shareholder in the company, was able to contribute a further £45,000, raising an extremely valuable £75,000 towards the outright purchase of a breast scanner for Frenchay Hospital in Bristol.

The Foundation also has a pro-active approach in the Third World and developing countries and has supported schemes in Uganda, Zimbabwe, Kenya, India, Nepal, Mozambique as well as maintaining a steady flow of donations to charities based in the UK.

The sheer size of the WTB Group makes the designation of it as a 'family firm' impossible; nevertheless there is a third generation member of the Burden family in a key position in the company. Today Jeremy Burden, the grandson of the founder, is Managing Director of WT Burden.

Against the current construction industry backdrop of consolidation and rationalisation the company is very proud of its independent status believing it to be a safeguard for customer choice against restrictive practices and a foundation for further growth.

The company occupies a prominent position in the industry but no-one's taking this for granted. It regularly exhibits at the major events in the construction industry. In this way the company profile is being raised and the range of products and extent of expertise is demonstrated to prospective clients and partners.

Though the company does not have a High Street presence, its products are used on and under the very streets we walk, and nowhere is this truer than Bristol and its surrounding areas. WTB Group will no doubt continue to make its own unique contribution to the environment around us, supplying products which make our towns and cities both more attractive and safer to live in.

Above left: *An aerial view of the Wellsway, Keynsham branch.*
Left: *One of WT Burdens fleet, loading up.*

A friend in need

All of us are familiar with insurance and the names of the handful of multi billion pound companies which dominate that market. And yet there are many smaller organisations with at least as much experience in the field - and moreover ones which do not have to hand over a large part of their profit to an army of shareholders before the poor policy holders get their bonuses.

One such 'mutual' organisation is the Bristol based National Deposit Friendly Society Ltd located in Worcester Road, Clifton.

The Friendly Society movement as we know it today has its roots in Scotland nearly 500 years ago, but the term Friendly Society was not in common use until the late 18th century.

The oldest established and longest lived association operating on Friendly Society principles was the Incorporation of Carters of Leith which survived for almost 500 years. In England the Poor Law Statute of 1601 gave some assistance to the poor and the sick - though not to immigrants. The many Huguenot refugees who came to England in the 17th century were not eligible for these early state benefits and in 1687 they formed one of the earliest Friendly Societies in England, originally known as the Society of Parisians, which survived until the early 20th century. The founder of the National Deposit Friendly Society was himself of Huguenot descent.

The first statute to give Friendly Societies legal recognition was an Act of 1793 which defined such organisations as 'societies of good fellowship for the purpose of raising from time to time, by voluntary contributions, a stock or fund for the material relief and maintenance of all and every one of the members thereof, in old age, sickness and infirmity, or for the relief of widows and children of deceased members'.

In pre-National Insurance days sickness amongst the working population almost inevitably meant loss of earnings. And for those who had neglected to put something by for the day of burial there was only a pauper's grave. To millions a pauper's grave was almost tantamount to dishonouring

Above: *The Rev.Canon George Raymond Portal, founder of the National Deposit Friendly Society.*
Right: *The first London office of the NDFS.*
Bottom left: *Albury Rectory where in 1868 the NDFS was born.*

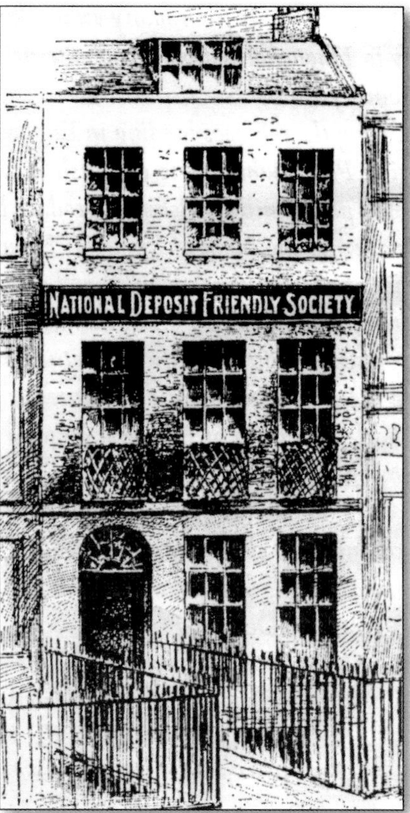

the dead. As time went by, in addition to sickness and death benefits, Friendly Societies began to offer other benefits such as hospital treatment, surgical appliances, dentures, spectacles, pensions, life assurance, group sickness insurance and loans.

The aim of every Friendly Society is to provide members with a fund upon which they or their dependants can call on in times of hardship due to illness, accident or death. They were and still are non-profit making organisations, and their original principles remain in place.

The origins of the National Deposit Friendly Society Ltd go back to 1868. In January of that year the Reverend Canon George Portal and three like minded worthies, John Pares, William Rock Carling and David Williamson, formed the Society as the Surrey County Deposit Benefit Club during a meeting at the vicarage at Albury just outside Guildford. The first committee meeting, and hence the official start date for the Society, would be on 20th April 1868. Originally called the Surrey County Deposit Benefit Club the 'club' had become 'Society' by its second meeting on 18th May 1868 by which time it had acquired its first 12 members, the very first of whom was a Mr A Humphreys. By the end of the year there were 191 members and the Society had acquired assets of £346 9s 4d.

Expansion was rapid and within three years members were to be found in all the counties surrounding Surrey. It was recognised that the Society would inevitably go nationwide and the name was changed to the National Deposit Friendly Society in 1871.

Over the next 20 years, from an initial membership of 12, membership had grown to almost 7,000 by the time of the Founder's death in April 1889. Ten years later membership had shot up to 35,000.

At the Annual Meeting of the Society in 1912 a motion that the National Deposit should expand to Canada was defeated by only 10 votes - if it had been passed the name would have become the International Deposit!

Expansion in the United Kingdom became even more rapid following the introduction of State Benefits (to be administered by Friendly Societies) in the National Insurance Act of 1911. As a direct result the National Deposit Friendly Society attracted more than 450,000 new members in the first six months - 350,000 because insured workers were now legally required to join one of the officially recognised institutions, but another 100,000 also joined the deposit section of their own free will.

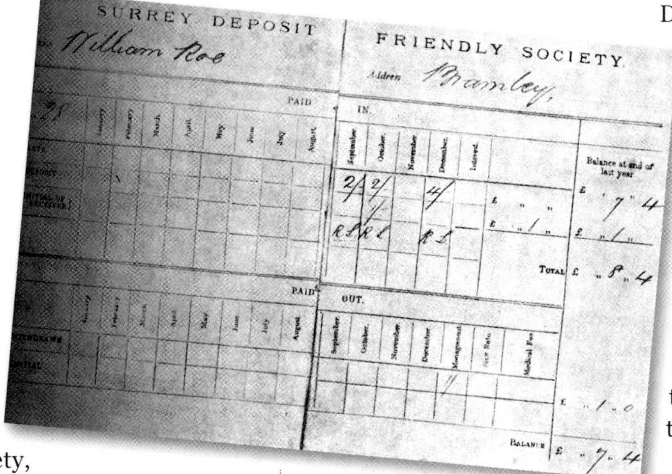
SURREY DEPOSIT FRIENDLY SOCIETY

William Roe

Address Bramley

PAID IN.

PAID OUT.

Top left: *The Society's Medals.* **Above left:** *The Hon. and Rev. Samuel Best, Canon of Winchester, originator of the Deposit System.* **Top right:** *Lewis Carroll author of 'Alice's Adventures in Wonderland, a life-long friend of Rev. Canon Portal.* **Above:** *An early balance book belonging to a customer of the Surrey Deposit Friendly Society.*

In the following decades progress was measured in tens of thousands of new members each year, the million mark being reached in the 1930s when membership was increasing at a rate of 100,000 annually.

National Deposit Friendly Society.

Guildford,
April 12th, 1880.

Sir,

The Annual General Meeting of the above Society will be held (Rule 12) at the Town Hall, Guildford, on Tuesday, April 27th, 1880, at 11-30 o'clock precisely, when you are invited to attend.

Members attending pay their own travelling expenses.

Please inform Delegate.

Yours faithfully,
J. MACFARLAND,
General Secretary.

These days few people remember life before the NHS, and even fewer are able to recall what life was like before the national insurance system came in as a result of the 1911 Act. Unless one had taken out private insurance incapacitating sickness meant poverty for the working man and the real threat of the workhouse. Surprisingly compulsory national insurance was not a British invention but a German one, introduced to Germany by the Iron Chancellor Otto von Bismark in the closing decades of the 19th century. Why was it introduced in Britain? One answer may have been fear that in the event of war the adult male population of the country might not have been healthy enough to join the armed forces; certainly the Government had been appalled to discover just how many potential recruits for the Boer War ten years earlier had failed to meet the fitness standards and been rejected by the army. Whatever the reasons however the United Kingdom's own Chancellor, Lloyd George, was of the view that a compulsory insurance system for workers which provided them with not only unemployment benefit but also the right to the free services of a GP and medicines might be a good idea.
Lloyd George despatched a young Treasury civil servant William Braithwaite off to Germany to investigate. After doing his research Braithwaite tracked the Chancellor down to the pier in Nice in the south of France where Lloyd George was apparently electioneering at a distance, there being a general election due the following week. The decision to go ahead with a national insurance scheme, with employees, employers and the state each paying a third of the cost, was made over tea on the pier. A new age was about to dawn - at least for workers - their wives and children would have to be considered later!

From today's perspective the arrangement seems quite odd, one does not expect state sickness benefit, payments to GPs and chemists or the payment of unemployment benefit to be paid by a non-Governmental organisation, but in 1911 this seemed a perfectly logical thing to do: the Government may have made National Insurance contributions compulsory but it simply did not have the infrastructure necessary to administer such a far reaching scheme - but

Above: *Notice of Annual Meeting in 1880.*
Below left: *The sixth Duke of Nothumberland and First President of the NDFS.* ***Below centre:*** *Author of 'Tom Brown's School Days' Thomas Hughes one of the NDFS's first trustees.* ***Below:*** *The Second London Office in Queen's Square from 1904-1923.*

Friendly Societies did. The State would use Friendly Societies and similar bodies to administer the new benefits without direct State administration of any kind until the late 1940s when the Government took over the work - an action which incidentally would eventually cost the NDFS over £200,000 in administrative expenses in respect of its 963,000 state members.

Before the inception of the NHS however the NDFS would introduce even more benefits for its members - not least convalescent homes. The Society became the first Approved Society to possess its own - and later build its own - convalescent home. Until 1920 the practice had been for the Society to come to an arrangement with the organiser of existing homes. The Society's first convalescent home of its own was opened in July 1920 at Dover overlooking St Margaret's Bay. Standing in its own grounds and four acres of gardens the home provided almost unlimited garden produce as well as tennis, bowls and sunbathing facilities. At its official opening the home was named Portal House. Portal House, named after the founder of the Society, was however open only to men. A second convalescent home, Everleigh Manor in Wiltshire, this time for women, was opened in 1921.

Left: *HRH the Duke of York the later King George VI opens the Society's Queens Square Office.*
Below: *The opening of the Skegness Memorial Home by HRH Princess Marie Louise.*

A third home would be opened in 1927, in Skegness, known as the Skegness Memorial Home, commemorating the 100,000 members of the Society who had died in the Great War of 1914-18. In 1937 yet another home opened, Aldingham Hall overlooking Morecambe Bay in Lancashire. During the second world war the homes were closed or requisitioned by the War Office and after the war were sold for other purposes - the Skegness Memorial Home for example becoming the local Town Hall in 1962, the year a new Portal House convalescent home would open in Bournemouth, the finest and most modern such home to be built in the UK up to that date. But that is to jump ahead of ourselves.

The Society's responsibilities in the area of administering State Benefits carried on right through to the implementation of the National Health Service Act in 1948; this brought about completely free medical treatment for all, not just for workers who paid for National Insurance Stamps. Many of the Society's staff were transferred to the NHS to help set up the new service.

The relationship between the Friendly Societies and Government had not always been easy. Inevitably the Societies had striven to preserve their independence and equally inevitably Government ministers had striven to curb it. In 1948 the Government released all Societies and other organisations from the duty of administering National Health Insurance and consequently from their other obligations under the Act.

Whilst the public may have welcomed the coming of the 'Welfare State' it threatened disaster for the Friendly Societies; their reason for existence seemed to have ended. By the end of 1949 278,206 members, especially the women and children who had not been insured under the old State scheme, had ceased to be members of the Society in the belief that because of the new NHS they would no longer need the NDFS to pay their doctors' bills.

A new role was needed for Friendly Societies, and life insurance, first introduced by the NDFS in 1900 was pushed to the fore along with endowment policies. A sales drive was put into place for the purpose of selling life insurance. Over 23,000 policies were in force within a few years representing nearly £1.75 million in sums assured and a premium income of £73,000.

Below left: *NDFS's Brunswick Square Property.*
Below: *The former head office of the NDFS.*

The growth of that section of business can be measured by the fact that in the 18 years, ending in 1966, the fund had grown from £221,000 to £2.25 million; the premium income from £19,687 to £265,330; the sums assured from £480,000 to £7.25 million and the number of policy holders from 17,661 to 47,282.

Since then the assets of the Society have increased progressively and now exceed £135 million; not a huge sum perhaps compared to many organisations, but one of sufficient size to maintain confidence in the future and the service the Society offers through mutuality.

Mutuality means that the direction and future of the Society is determined entirely by its members. There are no shareholders, nor directors with large salaries and expense accounts, or any expenditure that cannot be fully justified to maintain the smooth running of the Society and the service it provides to its members.

Anyone who joins the Society can, if they wish, take an active part in its management. The members of the Committee of Management for example act in an unpaid capacity, giving up their own time on behalf of the entire membership with the sole aim of improving conditions and benefits and protecting the interests of their fellow members. How many commercial companies can claim that their management decisions are unaffected by vested interests and that they work solely in the interests of the their customers?

Investing in UK ordinary shares, fixed interest stock and property, the operation normally results in an annual surplus of funds which, as they have been ever since 1868, are passed back to members by way of the addition of bonuses to with profit policies or enhancement of benefits in relation to sickness, accident and medical schemes. The National Deposit Friendly Society Ltd has come a long way since its humble origins; it now offers members a wide range of savings and health insurance products ranging from tax exempt savings plans to cover children's university education to 'with profit bonds' as well as employee group-sickness and accident schemes.

Above: *NDFS's former Divisional Office at 32-34 Colston Street.* ***Bottom:*** *The NDFS's 2001 Head Office in Clifton, Bristol.*

Building Bristol

How does a small firm begun by a single Bristol jobbing builder come to expand its business to become a major contracting company carrying out projects costing up to £50,000,000? The answer, not surprisingly, is time and hard work - in this case more than three generations of hard work.

Pearce was founded by Charles Henry Pearce in Bristol in 1922 when he returned to the UK after spending 25 years as an engineer in the South African gold mining industry.

By the end of the millennium the Pearce Group would be enjoying an annual turnover of £210,000,000 and have some 600 employees. It would be busy changing the Bristol cityscape with such projects as the Engineering and Office complex in Park Row, the six story building sited in the city centre to house the University's Faculty of Engineering as well as commercial offices and with the facade of a former cinema incorporated into it. Another prestigious building was Trinity Quay Phase II in Avon Street where a seven storey air conditioned office building with basement car parking would be built on a fast track programme, the building would feature the highest quality materials with extensive use of large precast stone cornices and arches to reflect the harbourside architecture. But such £10,000,000 projects were no doubt a long way from Charles Pearce's mind in 1922.

Charles' father had run a horse-drawn coach service between Westbury-on-Trym and Blackboy Hill during the second half of the 19th century. When Charles started as a jobbing builder his first workshop was in his father's stables at the top of Westbury Hill, but there were no horses for him - his first transport was a handcart. It would not be long however before Pearce lorries would become a familiar sight on the region's roads.

Charles Pearce soon moved into building houses in Westbury-on-Trym, Combe Dingle and Henleaze, and from 1926 he would have his son Gordon working with him. The company gradually expanded and during the second world war was

Top left: *Founder, Charles Henry Pearce.*
Below: *Pearce's first premises, Westbury Hill, Bristol.*

involved in defence work on military camps and establishments in the South West. From the mid-1950s the man at the helm was Gordon Pearce working in tandem with his brother Kenneth. They were later joined by long time stalwart Bernard Cripps followed by their respective sons, Derek and Tim Pearce. Mike Pearce, Gordon's youngest son would eventually be the last family member to work for the firm. Although the early 1950s were made difficult by the rationing of building materials the end of the decade would see the beginnings of a sustained boom in the building industry.

Over the years the company has moved the location of its headquarters, first from Westbury-on-Trym to Southmead Road where its old yard and office complex is now a police station; it then moved to its current headquarters at Parklands, Stoke Gifford. The ten acre Stoke Gifford site would prove to be a major asset to the company not only allowing for expansion but also being highly convenient for the M4/M5 junction and the Bristol Parkway railway station.

The company went public in 1968, with its shares quoted on the London Stock Exchange. It adopted a group logo in the form of three jig-saw pieces which Gordon Pearce chose because it symbolised the bringing together of those diverse talents and materials that are the essence of the construction industry.

By the time of the firm's diamond jubilee in 1984 Gordon and Kenneth Pearce had seen their father's firm which they had joined as young men grow from having a handful of employees to having 850 workers and from being a small jobbing builders to a group of 15 companies engaged in building

Top left: *Trinity Quay, Phase II, Avon Street, Bristol.* ***Above right:*** *An early Pearce project dating back to 1975, the Refuge Assurance Building, Baldwin Street, Bristol.* ***Right:*** *Pearce employee's from the early years.*

of vehicle; after some fruitless enquiries they were put in touch with Mr L Cullimore of Charfield who had an old lorry stored in a shed on his farm. The lorry was in exactly the kind of condition one might expect from having been hidden at the back of a barn for decades.

The vehicle was in a terribly dilapidated condition when Pearce bought it. It had to be completely dismantled down to the bare chassis and rebuilt . Many parts had to be manufactured. Every item was completely rebuilt, with the help of the Small Works Department helping with the body and cab seats. The task took a full year with many delays waiting for the manufacture of parts; but on completion the vehicle was as near as possible to the original as Pearce could make it.

One of the more visible aspects of the prescence of Pearce in their areas of operation was the Hot Air Balloon, which was used as a client marketing tool.

Above left: *The restored Ford Model B.* ***Below:*** *Engineering and office complex, Park Row, Bristol.* ***Below left:*** *The Pearce Balloon.*

activities from houses and extensions and decorating to multi-million pound industrial and commercial contracts. With companies specialising in electrical contracting, heating , plumbing, suspended ceilings, partitions and fire protection, plant and transport hire, shopfitting and office refurbishment Pearce would cover every aspect of construction. Pearce were also one of the first construction companies to employ design staff being able to offer a design and build service taking a job from the first thought stage through to total completion. Notable contracts which had by then been completed included a £7.8 million Hewlett Packard manufacturing facility at Stoke Gifford, a £7 million shop and office development in London's Kings Road and a £1.7 million new office development at Bristol's Bull Wharf.

To commemorate the firm's 60 years in business the directors found and renovated a Ford Model B truck of the kind which Charles Pearce had used in the early days of the business. Pearce instigated a national treasure hunt for this kind

In addition CH Pearce Construction Ltd now provides a service to the group for its commercial developments; it is also used as a research and development company to test new markets and to provide a service to selected Bristol and South West region clients. Two of the historic Pearce acquisitions continue in Evesham and Barnstaple.

Charles Henry Pearce would hardly recognise the company he formed with his sons all those years ago. Today the former jobbing building company is firmly established as one of the top twenty construction companies in the United Kingdom having been taken to the pinnacle of the building industry by Charles' successors.

In 1985 CH Pearce & Sons (Contractors) Ltd merged with Crest Nicholson PLC. At the time it was the largest construction company in the South West region. The company undertook any type of building construction work and any value of contract - carrying out works from major contracts down to what was still quaintly known as 'jobbing'.

One of the largest projects undertaken by Pearce was the 800,000 sq ft Colour Television Manufacturing Facility, for Sony in Bridgend. This project was undertaken and completed within a 56 week period for the value of £25,000,000.

The company was organised on a regional basis with three main regions: the South West, the South East and the Midlands, with a small office in North Devon.

The geographic boundaries that were created by a regional structure worked well for some time but eventually a change of strategy was needed - nation-wide clients required nation-wide teams not different teams depending on region or value. Such major clients would come to include the likes of the AA, ASDA, the BBC, IBM, Rolls Royce, Shell, Sony, Tesco, Whitbread, Zeneca and many, many other well known businesses and institutions.

Since 1996 Pearce has moved away from being a general provider of construction services to being a specialist provider. This has been done by forming autonomous specialist business units each with its own specialist skills and with dedicated focused management.

These businesses specialise in Retail, Leisure and Clean Room Technology Sectors.

But family values and traditions, so important in the past, are still a key ingredient in the company's approach to business, complemented now by modern styles of management and the stability of corporate status. The story of Pearce is a remarkable one and an inspiration to the present generation of young entrepreneurs. Huge success may take time to achieve, but Charles Pearce demonstrated that it is possible for one man or woman imbued with the work ethic and inspired by what is possible to turn what was once not even a one-horse operation into a vast and prestigious company.

Top: *The colour television manufacturing facility for Sony.* ***Below:*** *The Pearce Complex, Parklands, Bristol.*

An act of faith

Opened in 1766, Bristol's historic Theatre Royal is the oldest continuously working theatre in England. It is also one of the first playhouses in the country to be based on a horseshoe-shaped auditorium (inspired by the original Theatre Royal, Drury Lane), setting a trend followed by theatre builders for generations to come.

Impetus for the construction of the Theatre Royal came from the city's business community, with 49 wealthy merchants contributing £50 each towards construction costs. In return for their investment, each was entitled to a silver token allowing them a free sight of every performance on the Theatre Royal stage. A number of these tokens remain in existence today, and are still honoured at the box office.

However, far from being a respectable cornerstone of society, theatre in Georgian England was considered by the Bristol city fathers to 'encourage wickedness' and plans to build the Theatre Royal were disparaged in print as 'at risk of ruining the morals of our youth, impoverishing our tradesmen and artisans and diffusing a habit of idleness, indolence and debauchery throughout this industrious and virtuous city.'

None of this deterred the merchants who, after all, had sought to build the theatre for purely commercial reasons.

Right: *The interior of the Theatre Royal in the 1960s.*
Below: *An artists view of the Theatre Royal in Victorian times.*

This resulted in the Theatre Royal acquiring not only its regal title but also the distinctive coat of arms which is still displayed today. Plays could, at last, be staged legitimately.

They made their investment back with handsome dividends on top within 30 years of opening.

Ingenious loopholes came into play allowing the theatre to function in its proper role as a playhouse. Plays were initially described as 'specimens of Rhetorick' to evade tight laws governing the performance of drama which had been introduced across England in 1737. The language used on posters and playbills was far more disingenuous than even today's hard-sell marketing jargon.

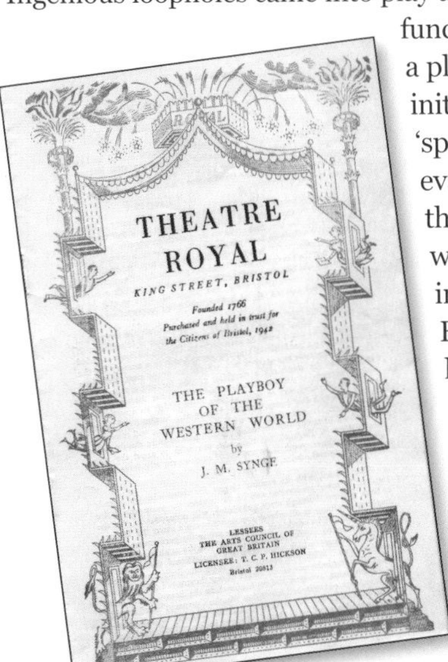

THEATRE ROYAL

KING STREET, BRISTOL

Founded 1766

Purchased and held in trust for the Citizens of Bristol, 1942

THE PLAYBOY OF THE WESTERN WORLD

by

J. M. SYNGE

LESSEES THE ARTS COUNCIL OF GREAT BRITAIN

LICENSEE: T. C. F. HICKSON

In order to lawfully stage plays, theatres had to apply for the Royal Patent, which was bestowed on the Theatre Royal in 1778, making it one of only five or six venues outside London to be so designated. (Bath, for many years run in tandem with Bristol, was one of the first in this respect).

Originally, the Theatre Royal had a capacity of 1,000 and staged productions only in the spring and summer. This increased to 1,600 with the reconstruction of the roof and extension of the gallery in the early nineteenth century. Some of this original bench seating can still be seen today (although, in the interests of comfort, it is no longer offered as seating to paying customers).

It is as well that the capacity was so substantial because at the time, it was capable of attracting every great name in British theatre. Edmund Kean, Robert Baddeley, Sarah Siddons and the famous clown Grimaldi were all regular performers on the famous stage.

But, as the nineteenth century progressed, it was the Macready dynasty that became synonymous with the theatre's success. The patriarch of this famous family was William McCready (properly M'Cready), the larger-than-life son of a Dublin upholsterer, a Freemason and regular visitor to the bankruptcy courts.

Top right: *Peter O'Toole appearing in Hamlet in 1958.*
Top left: *Maggie Smith and Robert Hardy in the Bristol Old Vic production of The Rehearsal in 1961.*
Left: *A programme for the production of The Playboy of the Western World.*

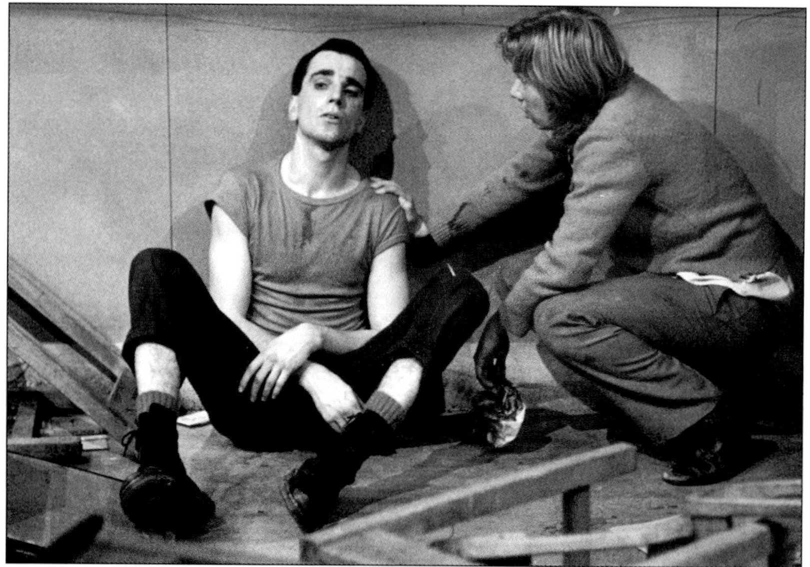

became the next to manage the Theatre Royal. And it was he who faced the stiffest task, as the building of substantial new residential suburbs in the west of the city saw King Street become a far from fashionable part of the city centre - and nobody's idea of the right place for a good night out.

Responding to this trend, Chute opened the Princes' Theatre on Park Row in 1867. This theatre prospered as the Theatre Royal's fortunes declined, a state of affairs which was to last for much of the early twentieth century.

One problem was the increasingly prohibitive running costs of the building, now more than a century old. Before the advent of gas and electricity, oil lamps and tallow candles were used for lighting, with obvious effects on the appearance of the interior. The wooden benches became old and uncomfortable. The newer, plusher rival in Park Row had the upper hand.

Little work of significant artistic merit was produced for many years in King Street, and this was accompanied by a long period of financial uncertainty until the theatre was finally put up for auction in 1942.

It would have been in keeping with the prevailing economic situation if the theatre had been lost as a playhouse at that time. Many similar venues ceased their activity during wartime, pushed into emergency use in support of the war effort, and never to recover their artistic usage. But intervention by the Council for the Preservation of Ancient Bristol saved the day, and they paid £10,500 for

McCready senior took over the running of the Theatre Royal in 1819, and brought with him his mistress, the actress Sarah Desmond. Upon their marriage and the eventual death of her husband in 1829, Sarah Macready began the process of relinquishing her acting career for theatrical management.

For two decades, she ran the Theatre Royal with a rod of iron, evoking fear and admiration from those who worked with her. Running a theatre in those days was not considered to be the usual profession of Victorian ladies.

The Theatre Royal in those days was as famous for the characters it produced as much as the historic importance of the building. Actors regularly risked life and limb in garish productions featuring wild animals. The legendary violinist Paganini played here. A tightrope walker, Il Diavolo Antonio duelled in Queen Square with the actor Mr Booth, in a dispute over Antonio's wife. In the mid-nineteenth century, it could be said of the Theatre Royal that there was as much drama off stage as on it.

Macready's son, William Charles, was to become one of the most distinguished actors of his generation. But it was her son-in-law James Henry Chute who

Top left: *Daniel Day Lewis in the production of Class Enemy, 1980.* ***Right:*** *Kevin Whately, Tony Haygarth, Timothy West, Peter Vaughan, Tim Healy and Stuart Rayner in the Bristol Old Vic's production of Twelve Angry Men, directed by Harold Pinter, 1996.*

the building, which was promptly put into trust status, which it retains today.

To mark the relaunch of the Theatre Royal, the famous Old Vic company from London was invited to stage a production. It put on Goldsmith's She Stoops To Conquer, featuring Dame Sybil Thorndike as Mrs Hardcastle. This production was to prove a defining moment in the modern history of the Theatre Royal.

Upon the end of World War Two, the Old Vic was invited to set up a permanent sister company in the city, and the Bristol Old Vic came into being.

The company's first production - a revival of The Beaux' Stratagem - was staged on February 19, 1946. It marked the beginning of a golden era for what was to become Britain's most famous regional theatre company.

With the parallel founding of the Bristol Old Vic Theatre School, the Theatre Royal offered the first professional opportunities to many of the great British actors of the recent past - Peter O'Toole, Paul Eddington, Brian Blessed, Patricia Routledge, Pete Postlethwaite, Jeremy Irons, Daniel Day-Lewis and Miranda Richardson among them.

The company was associated with some of the great theatrical productions of the time. Julian Slade's classic musical Salad Days was premiered in 1954. Beryl Reid and Eileen Atkins shared the billing in the first ever staging of The Killing of Sister George.

In 1963, Bristol Old Vic became independent from its sister company in London, as the original Old Vic company was dissolved and reconstituted as the National Theatre.

Further refurbishment took place in the early seventies, leading to the construction of the New Vic Studio.

Today, Bristol Old Vic remains one of the top theatre companies in Britain. It regularly works with the country's leading actors, most recently Tara Fitzgerald in A Streetcar Named Desire and Nick Moran in Look Back In Anger. Bristol Old Vic's productions are often seen on national tour, and many transfer to the West End.

Bristol Old Vic's most recent success, however, came not in the Theatre Royal, but at Princes Wharf in the heart of the City Docks. This was the scene of Up the Feeder, Down the Mouth And Back Again, a massive collaboration with Bristol Museums celebrating the city's maritime tradition.

In the immediate future, the company has two main goals: firstly to maintain its reputation for delivering 'world-class theatre, made in Bristol' - and secondly, to undertake a comprehensive refurbishment and restoration of the Theatre Royal complex, which remains today, as it has for more than two centuries, one of the crown jewels of British theatre.

***Top left:** Bristol Old Vic's production, Up The Feeder, Down The' Mouth And Back Again at Princes Wharf, July 2001. **Far left:** A side view of Bristol Old Vic. **Left:** The imposing facade of Bristol Old Vic.*

Ironmongery in the blood

One of Bristol's oldest businesses is Pattersons in Redcliffe Street which boasts up to 13,000 stock lines of cleaning, catering, gardening and ironmongery equipment. This long-lived firm was founded in the reign of Queen Victoria by a Devonshire man, Robert Patterson, and the firm he founded remains a family concern, run by his descendants, to this day.

Born in Uplyme, Devon, Robert Smith Patterson was the younger of the two sons of an Axminster cattle dealer; despite having suffered from infantile paralysis as a child Robert worked for several years for a manufacturer of diesel engines.

Robert's older brother, William Drew Patterson, decided to leave Devon and move to Bristol where he got a job in an ironmongery business at 10 Castle Street. William took over that business when his employer sold out in 1886.
As a result of his brother's initiative Robert came to work for William in Bristol. Soon their trade was too large for the premises to cope. With both brothers anxious to expand their business they agreed that the younger brother should be made sole owner of new premises which they bought from Thomas Hamilton Adams at 74 Redcliffe Hill. The valuer estimated the value of the stock at £1,081, a sum which was then made over to Mr Adams and the assignment of the lease ending in 1891 was completed for the sum of £70 per year payable to the feoffees of St Mary Redcliffe church. It was this division that was ultimately to launch the success of RS Patterson & Sons and eventually lead, in 1937, to the folding of WD Patterson & Son.

A regular trade was soon established by Robert Patterson with Bristol and Avonmouth docks, the General Hospital and with farmers and farriers from all over

Above: *Founder, Robert Patterson.*
Below: *Pattersons first shop in Redcliffe Hill.*

the west country; a trade which Robert was well prepared for after his early days in Devon. Every month he would collect orders to deliver goods to farmers as far away as Chard and Martock in Somerset, a journey which took several days at a time when the road surfaces were poor and a pony and trap was often the best transport available.

Back in Bristol, every Thursday was Market Day when farmers would flock to the town. Robert Patterson would display his wares outside the shop window and secure orders for the rest of the week before crossing the road to the crowded Hope & Anchor pub to conduct more business over a pint of ale.

The business grew steadily with the lease of the premises in Redcliffe Hill renewed in 1891 for £80 and again in 1905 for £85.

Despite inevitable hurdles life was looking good. In 1893 Robert married Mary Brice; by 1900 they had four children, Olive, Lillian, Henry (known as Harry) and Donald.

By lying about his age young Harry joined the cavalry during the first world war and served in Ireland. In 1918 rather than go into the ironmongery trade Harry wanted to become a tea planter in Ceylon but he was persuaded to join the family firm along with his younger brother Donald.

By 1930 Harry and Donald had sufficient experience for their father to make them junior partners.

It was just in time. Four years later, at the age of 77, and after 50 years in the business Robert Patterson died having continued working right up until his death.

One of the first moves the two sons made was to set up a stall in Winford market ten miles south of Bristol, renting a pitch there for £6 a year.

In 1937 WD Patterson & Son announced that they were in financial difficulties and unable to continue to trade. William Patterson its founder was by then over 80 and in poor health whilst his son Charles had little aptitude for the business. Harold and Donald therefore bought their uncle's business, which by then was being conducted from Cock & Bottle Lane.

Until shortly before Robert Patterson's death the horse and cart had still been the main means of delivering goods until a small box truck had been bought; this was replaced by a larger Bedford lorry in 1939 just before the outbreak of the second world war. That same year the brothers

Top: *Pattersons Guinea Street premises which was mainly used for storage.* ***Above:*** *An agreement for purchase of stock, 1889.*

bought 41 Guinea Street to the rear of Redcliffe Street. The new premises provided garaging, storage space and two underground petrol tanks.

With the outbreak of war the lorry was requisitioned by the army. No more was heard of the lorry until 1945 when the Patterson brothers received a letter and a photograph from the British Embassy in Belgrade: the lorry had been found in Yugoslavia by two Americans. Abandoned at Dunkirk the lorry had been repainted after being commandeered by the Germans until it had been abandoned; the Patterson name had shown through its burned paintwork.

Soon after the war Newicks ironmongery firm at 66 Redcliffe Hill went bankrupt and the brothers bought it. Then another firm, Harris & Kingdom in Victoria Street also got into difficulties and the brothers bought that too, though keeping the Harris & Kingdom name.

There was plenty of work to do. Fortunately by 1953 a new generation of Pattersons had joined the business in the the form of Harry's sons Bryan and Richard.

In 1960 additional premises were acquired when Sampsons furniture makers closed at 14 Victoria Street. More expansion followed when Fox & Vowles, which sold washroom and cleaning materials, was bought.

Sadly, in 1965, Harry Patterson suffered a stroke whilst driving, as result of the stroke and injuries susuatined in the ensuing accident he was unable to ever return to work. Just one year later Donald died of a sudden heart attack.

Top: *The Harris and Kingdom premises in Victoria Street.*
Above: *RS Pattersons on Redcliffe Hill in the 1930s.*

Harry's sons Bryan and Richard took over the businesses. One of the first steps they took was to look for new premises to combine the whole business under one roof, a move made all the more urgent by a pending compulsory purchase of 74 Redcliffe Hill for road widening. In 1969 a move was made to 30-36 Redcliffe Street, the site at which the company is still based.

The following year Pattersons acquired the retail business of Gaskell & Chambers, a firm which provided pubs with such items as glasses and bar supplies. Coupling that business with existing sales of cleaning materials Pattersons was soon nominated sole supplier to a hundred or more managed pubs in the south west. The catering supply side of the business would eventually grow to become the largest part of the firm's business.

In 1981 Christopher Patterson, Bryan's son joined the firm from Marks & Spencer, where he had been since graduating from Cambridge University.

Times were changing all round. The agricultural industry no longer seemed to be using fastenings and small tools in the way it had in earlier times. The agricultural division of Pattersons was closed in 1985 along with the market stall - sales were still good but margins were too small. The released capital was put into catering supplies and by 1989 this had become the major part of the firm's business.

In that centenary year Pattersons bought out Hardware (Bristol) Ltd which supplied retail shops, holiday camps and Berni Inns with catering supplies. In order to cope with the increase in business Pattersons increased its warehouse space by 6,000 sq. ft.

In 1990 Bryan Patterson became the first member of his family to actually retire. Three years later Richard Patterson also retired leaving the firm, for the first time in almost 70 years, in the hands of just one family member, Bryan's son Christopher.

Pattersons are looking forward to a future of continued growth. The year 2001 saw the company return to the home county of Robert Patterson with the opening of a second branch in Exeter. Now, with an annual turnover of more than £7 million and a staff of more than 70, Pattersons can look back at a past which would have astonished Robert Patterson when he first left his home in Devon so many years ago to seek his fortune in Bristol.

Above left: *A view inside Pattersons.*
Below: *A staff photograph.*
Bottom: *Pattersons premises in Redcliffe Street.*

An en-gauging tale

Most of us are familiar with gauges and liquid level gauges in particular. You probably see one most days of your life when you check to see how much petrol you have left in your car. Or maybe you have oil fired central heating and there is a gauge attached to the side of the tank to enable you to read off how much heating oil you have left.

Knowing just how much petrol or oil we have is an important part of managing our day to day lives, but for industry the ability to measure far larger quantities is vital. One local firm, Seetru, which has specialised in this aspect of the industrial world.

And the engineering problems involved do not simply concern measurements; they also involve valve engineering and handling potentially dangerous liquids safely.

Answering questions like that of a Marine Engineer wishing to know the contents of his fuel oil, lubrication oil and water tanks is exactly what Seetru offers.

Right: *Seetru Works, when situated under the Arches at Temple Meads Station.* ***Below:*** *Founder Leonard Taylor covering the standing start kilometre at Silverstone in a time of 45.03 seconds, driving a 1911 10hp Stanley Steam Car, 1949.*

Similarly Seetru has devised measuring gauges for use in the huge vats used by the brewing and distilling industries to enable their contents to be read easily and hygienically, and to an accuracy which will not only satisfy the Customs and Excise but also ensure perfect stock control.

Seetru Limited, now based at the Albion Dockside Works, Hanover Place, is the main company within a small group of subsidiary and associated companies: East Bristol Engineers Limited, Ebtrade Limited (a subsidiary of East Bristol

Engineers) and Paxend a division of Seetru. All the parts of the group work together in an integrated fashion.

Seetru Limited was founded in 1949 and incorporated as a limited company on 13th October of that year. Following its establishment it began developing and exploiting engineering ideas in liquid level gauging, valve engineering and resilient fastening methods for machinery and equipment.

The period was one of optimism following the ending of the second world war in 1945. The economy was just beginning an upsurge which, though folk did not then know it, would last for twenty years or more. The pent up energies of many young men, and older ones, had been held in check by six years of war followed by a period of austerity. That pent up enterprise would be released in a surge as thousands upon thousands of young vital businesses would be started, and though many would fall by the wayside many others would survive to grow into major undertakings.

The firm of Seetru Ltd was founded by Leonard Taylor who had previously worked in the oil distribution business; he set out to supply level gauges for 40 gallon oil drums from premises in Queen Square. In 1950 Leonard Taylor was joined by Otto Varga whose son, Dr Andrew Varga, is now also involved in the business. From having simply distributed gauges the firm began to develop its own level gauging

This Page: *Seetru's third offices in the basement of the historic Bristol Commercial Rooms.*

devices for industry. Subsequently the company would begin to produce fluid valve products, especially safety valves from mainly brass and stainless steel.The company created the Touchtite sealing system for safety valves which presented a totally new level of performance in this field of engineering.

The small but growing firm would stay at its original premises for just six years before making the first of several moves: the offices were moved initially to Stokes Croft and the Workshop to Temple Meads Arches; subsequently offices would move to the basement of the historic Bristol Commercial Rooms in Corn Street and the factory to Cumberland Road. Albion Dockside Works was opened in 1980 in the re-built engine works of Charles Hill's Bristol Shipyard. Eventually in 2000 the Cumberland Road site was sold and the factory transferred to the enlarged and further modernised Albion Dockside Works.

From its small beginnings, when all manufacturing was subcontracted, the group of companies steadily built up its capacity for manufacture and by the millennium would have a turnover of over £5 million and employ 120 staff at two factories in the docks area. Although relatively small in size Seetru had become a comprehensive, vertically integrated engineering enterprise comprising sales and marketing, design and development, production and administration. The production department would have the most up to date machining facilities and utilise the most modern organisational practices with all aspects of the operation supported by extensive and up to date information technology systems.

The gradual growth of the company over more than fifty years would depend upon the development and perfection of its gauge and valve products, especially in the field of safety valves. By the millennium the firm had extended its business into the field of coded pipe couplings based on a patented range of coded pipe coupling systems.

The company reputation would be enhanced by an ethos of engineering excellence and great attention to customers' needs. The firm would also operate a substantial development test plant for safety valves and additionally have environmental test facilities for all its products.

From its earliest beginnings Seetru had a special interest in exports, for example in liquid level gauges for the marine and shipbuilding industries. The company would continue to strengthen and expand its international position in Europe and elsewhere, not least the important Far East trade, even granting limited manufacturing licences in Japan.

The company also manufactures safety relief and other special purpose ancillary valves for a wide range of compressed air, industrial gas, dust, steam and liquid applications which meet all important international standards.

Seetru also has a range of special purpose valves which are largely for the compressed air industry and for medium sized industrial oil engines. These products include minimum pressure maintaining valves for screw type compressors and air starting valves for medium sized industrial and marine oil engines.

Seetru liquid level gauges are primarily three types: sight gauges, magnetic gauges and capsule operated types.

Top left and right: *The Albion Dockside Works extension under construction.* ***Above:*** *A Seetru cartoon.*

Many of the gauges are direct reading, though Seetru also offers a variety of pneumatic and electronic remote reading systems too.

The gauge range notably includes the Quickmount and CPI gauges for industrial and chemical applications as well as the Seetol system for tall tanks (to 20 metres and above) which incorporate optical and close circuit TV viewing systems.

The Seetru range of gauges for marine applications have for many years been the workhorses of the Marine industry, being approved by all the important classification organisations such as Lloyds Register of Shipping, Germanischer Lloyd, NKK Japan, ABS and Det Norske Veritas.

A recent addition to Seetru's product range has been its patented coded pipe coupling system which provides safety and security in pipe and hose coupling for liquid and gas transfer. Such couplings ensure that only predetermined, correct couplings can be made whilst maintaining existing pipe and hosework practice.

The company provides reconditioning and maintenance services as well as a design advisory service - helping to develop or adapt individual products to new applications in industry. The company has a full Design and Development Department with significant test facilities to adapt its own products, to develop new ones and also to undertake design and development work for its customers.

Seetru provides training courses covering the use and maintenance of its own and similar products. In particular this may concern the specification, installation, operation and maintenance of safety valves, for instance in the light of the European Pressure Systems directive.

The packing department of the company undertakes both packing and some direct transport services of its own products whilst the Paxend division provides a range of packing and despatch services for outside customers on a contract basis.

Today Seetru's main markets are shipbuilders, railways, compressor manufacturers and chemical and process engineers. The firm has come a long way from its first product, those gauges to measure the contents of 40 gallon oil drums. But the world moves on and as it does so its demands become ever more complex: valves, joints and seals which were deemed adequate forty, twenty or even ten years ago no longer meet the evermore stringent standards required in an increasingly safety conscious world. And rightly so, the scale of industrial enterprises grows ever larger and with that growth in size and increase in danger. Only by keeping pace with such changes across the whole range of engineering science can we ensure that the world of tomorrow is not only bigger and better but that it is also a safer one. Seetru Limited promises to deliver under all those headings.

Top left: *A view inside Seetru Ltd.*
Above right: *A staff photograph.*
Below: *Albion Dockside Works before the addition of the new extension.*

Mixing oil with sand

Millions of motorists have seen the name 'Silvey Services' on the M32. But who or what is Silvey?

Thomas Silvey and Company was founded in 1870 by, the then thirty year old, Thomas Silvey; he had been working for the Gloucester Railway and Carriage Company which built railway rolling stock and he had seen that money was being made by the owners of private wagon fleets. The coal trade was by far the largest user of railway wagons and Thomas felt that as a coal merchant he would be best able to use his expertise in operating such a fleet.

At that time coal was almost the sole source of energy and the new firm soon began to supply coal to public utilities, industry and domestic consumers. At that time utilities were either privately owned or controlled by Local Authorities. Early customers were the gas companies at Bristol, Bath, Bridgwater, Thornbury, Dursley and most of the Cotswold towns.

Amongst industrial customers were United Alkali (later part of ICI), Georges Brewery (now Courage), the Distillers Company, St Anne's Board Mills, Frys and other chocolate companies as well as various soft drink bottlers. Bacon curers in Wiltshire and the local brickworks of Somerset and Gloucestershire were all served by direct company sidings or by road using horses and carts.

In 1878 Tom's second son, Gilbert Ernest Silvey, was born; he was educated at the Merchant Venturers School in Bristol and had ambitions to become a banker. His elder brother, Frank, worked for Spillers and Baker (later Dalgety) so the younger boy was persuaded to join the coal business and eventually succeeded his father in 1900 when the older man died at the age of sixty. At that time Frank Silvey, seeing the success of the coal business elected to leave Spillers and join the family firm. It was a mistake, as might have been foreseen. There was friction between the brothers for while the youngest, Gilbert, had the experience and was in control his elder brother was not prepared to accept a subordinate role. The end result was that Frank Silvey left to set up a competing business at Fishponds.

Because many industrial customers were sited on docks in the Bristol Channel, Gilbert Silvey built up a fleet of small sailing colliers carrying coal from the Welsh and Forest of Dean coal fields. By the end of the 1914-18 war these were being replaced by motor vessels: the first was the MV Nigel, which although built as a landing craft for the Gallipoli campaign never reached that theatre of war.

Gilbert Silvey's first son, Thomas Silvey, had been born in 1912; he was educated at Wycliffe College, Stonehouse and joined the firm in 1930, four years after the prolonged miners' strike of 1926. At the time young Thomas joined his father the firm had, by then, become the sole agents in the South West for a number of collieries, then privately owned, in various coalfields.

Top left: *Gilbert Ernest Silvey, son of the company founder.* ***Above right:*** *Gilbert Silvey's wife, Sylvia, launching the MV Wycliffe in 1949.* ***Right:*** *A delivery for the coal boiler circa 1953, Midland Road.*

In 1934 Gilbert Silvey died and his place was taken by Sam Colburn. In the following year Bryan, GE Silvey's youngest son, also joined the business. Improvements to the fleet continued: in 1939 the MV Denby was built for the firm at the Bristol yard owned by Charles Hill.

In 1940, following the outbreak of World war II, the business was incorporated and Thomas Lindsay Silvey was appointed a director of the company. In that same year the new company took an interest in a new tugboat company called Bristol Towages Ltd of which Thomas was also to become a founding director. And also in that year TL Silvey's first son, Thomas Michael, was born and like his father would later be educated at Wycliffe College. TL Silvey served in the RAF from 1943 until 1946 when he was demobbed as Flight Lieutenant. In that year he and his brother Bryan became joint Managing Directors of the company.

Troubled times lay ahead. In 1948 the company's fleet of railway wagons now numbering several hundred was nationalised for the sum of just £13,747. In the same year however the company acquired a fifty per cent holding in Bristol Towages Ltd. The other half of that company was bought by Renwick, Wilton & Dobson Ltd (later part of Western Fuel). And in the following year Charles Hill built the MV Wycliffe, a sister ship of the MV Denby, for the company.

In 1951 Sam Colburn died and was succeeded by Thomas L Silvey as Chairman. In 1954, encouraged by bank interest rates of just 4.5 percent, the company entered the oil trade as a distributor for Petrofina.

The future was in oil and by 1963 the coal trade had changed, the MV Nigel, though still going strong, was chartered 'bareboat' to a contractor involved in the development of the Milford Haven oil refineries. Meanwhile the company by this time was operating a number of coal distribution depots in Bristol, Gloucester and Wiltshire.

In 1964 the MV Nigel, now equipped as a sand dredger, was reported adrift in the Irish Sea. A dispute with the charter party followed because the dredger was operating outside her

Top left: *The company's first purpose built tanker, acquired after becoming an authorised distributor for Petrofina in 1955.* ***Top right:*** *Silvey's showed their support for the Bristol University Rags by entering floats in their carnivals throughout the 1950s.* ***Above right:*** *Mr Thomas Silvey pictured in 1963 whilst President of the Coal Merchants Federation of GB.* ***Right:*** *Marketing of the new Coalite fuel and it's daily delivery service by Thomas Silvey in 1939. The first recipient pictured here is actress Jean Colin, who was appearing in pantomime at the Prince's Theatre.*

insurance limits. The matter being unresolved, one dark night, a crew from the company repossessed the boat at Milford Haven and sailed her to Bristol. As she was now in company possession the dispute was resolved and MV Nigel was chartered to Bristol Towages Ltd. That company now started operations as a sand dredging business and later changed its name to Sand Supplies (Western) Ltd.

In 1962 Silvey's turnover exceeded £1 million for the first time. When in 1963 TL Silvey was elected President of the Coal Merchants Federation Great Britain he became involved in negotiations with Alf (later Lord) Robens and transport minister Dr Beeching in the 'rationalisation' of the railways; an event which resulted in a tremendous change in the coal trade. In 1966 Thomas Michael Silvey who had been working in Australia and Japan joined the company which had now begun to concentrate its distribution activities on sites away from the railways in Gloucestershire, Somerset and South Wales.

In 1970 the business of FH Silvey & Co Ltd, founded by Frank Silvey, was amalgamated with Thomas Silvey Ltd and shortly afterwards Bryan Silvey retired as director.

Top left: *Staff from Malmesbury, Charfield and Badminton Coal Depots enjoying a coach outing.* ***Above right:*** *The opening of Silvey's and Bristol's first prepacked coal vending machine, Tom Silvey looks on (second from the left) with his brother Bryan behind his right shoulder.* ***Below:*** *The firm's suction dredger, Sand Diamond a converted Norwegian bulk carrier, passing through the lock to enter the floating harbour at Cumberland Basin.*

The Head Office was moved from Midland Road to Surrey Street in 1971. In 1973 it acquired the 50 percent equity held by Renwick, Wilton & Dobson in Sand Supplies (Western) Ltd which now became a wholly owned subsidiary. The Head Office was again moved in 1976 to 101-119 Newfoundland Road, a site which also included a filling station.

In 1978 Thomas Michael Silvey was appointed Managing Director leaving TL Silvey to continue as Chairman. Three years later the first chain of FLARE petrol filling stations was commissioned by the Oil Division: that year turnover would exceed £10 million.

By 1985 after the miners' strike the company's Coal Division distribution amounted to less than 10 percent of turnover. By then more than fifty filling stations were under contract, and the sand dredging company had become the eighth largest in the UK. Turnover had reached an astonishing £20 million.
In 1986 the coal business was sold to Cawoods (a subsidiary of Redland) and the corporate plan was modified to expand the Oil Division's interest in filling stations and make this activity a separate profit centre.

Two years later TL Silvey died and the following year Sand Supplies (Western) Ltd was sold off enabling the company to concentrate on its main area of expertise.

In 1990 the company acquired Oakleigh Acres near Chippenham which it developed into a major truck bunkering and services facility. That same year the Wallace Arnold Coach station in Plymouth was bought to establish a Plymouth Truckstop there.

Still keeping the family links going after 175 years David Hatherell, TM Silvey's stepson, became Transport Manager in 1995 and was subsequently appointed General manager of the company's Fuel Marketing Centre.

In the late 1990s land, adjacent to the company's Head Office, was acquired for redevelopment. Under the direction of Project Manger, Scott Lord, demolition was carried out in March 1999 and that April MA Construction Ltd began building to the design of architect Kit Routledge and civil engineer Vic Webb.

The result was Silveys M32 Services, opened to the public on 8th August 1999 and in November 2000 the project received a design award presented by the Bristol Civic society.

***Top left:** Pictured at the opening of Silvey's M32 Services are Michael Silvey, his sister Diana Geraghty (Assistant Credit Manager) on his right, wife Diana (responsible for administering the company's fuel cards) to his left and stepson David Hatherell (Operations Director). **Left:** Sir Stirling Moss behind the wheel of his Jaguar helping to launch the new experimental 24hr unattended petrol station in 1987.Whilst this was not successful it did pave the way for unattended commercial filling stations at Llantrisant, Cwmgwili, Plympton, Bridgwater and Chippenham. **Right:** Michael Silvey, Managing Director. **Below:** Silvey's M32 Service station which opened in 1999.*

Chocolates fit for a queen

Say the name Elizabeth Shaw in Bristol and what do you think of? Delicious chocolates that's what. Bristol and chocolate have been inseparable in people's' minds for far beyond living memory and although the Elizabeth Shaw name only arrived in Bristol in the 1960s the firm, which makes that delicious range of liqueur chocolates and specialities, has local roots which go back to the 19th century.

The business was started in Bristol in 1881 trading under the name of HJ Packer. Packer had previously worked for Fry's of Bristol which was the first major chocolate producing firm in Bristol.

Packer began making chocolate in a house at 46, Armoury Square, Stapleton Road under the name of Packer & Co. The staff consisted of Packer's sister and brother, and a Miss Lily Brown who was paid half a crown a week. The plant was simple - a kitchen fire and a paraffin lamp provided the heat and light whilst two saucepans and a smaller pan were used for making the chocolate and the cream centres. Sugar was bought 14 lbs at a time and the finished chocolates were delivered by hand.

The following year saw increased demand and the number of staff was doubled; soon afterwards the business moved to larger premises in St Paul's Street.

In 1884 Packer took a partner - HJ Burrows - another former Fry's employee - whose initials were now incorporated in the title of the firm. The partnership

Right: *HRH Princess Elizabeth being presented with Elizabeth Shaw chocolates by Valerie Joyce, daughter of Elizabeth Shaw.* **Below:** *The unloading of cocoa mass, sugar and cocoa butter in the early 1900s.*

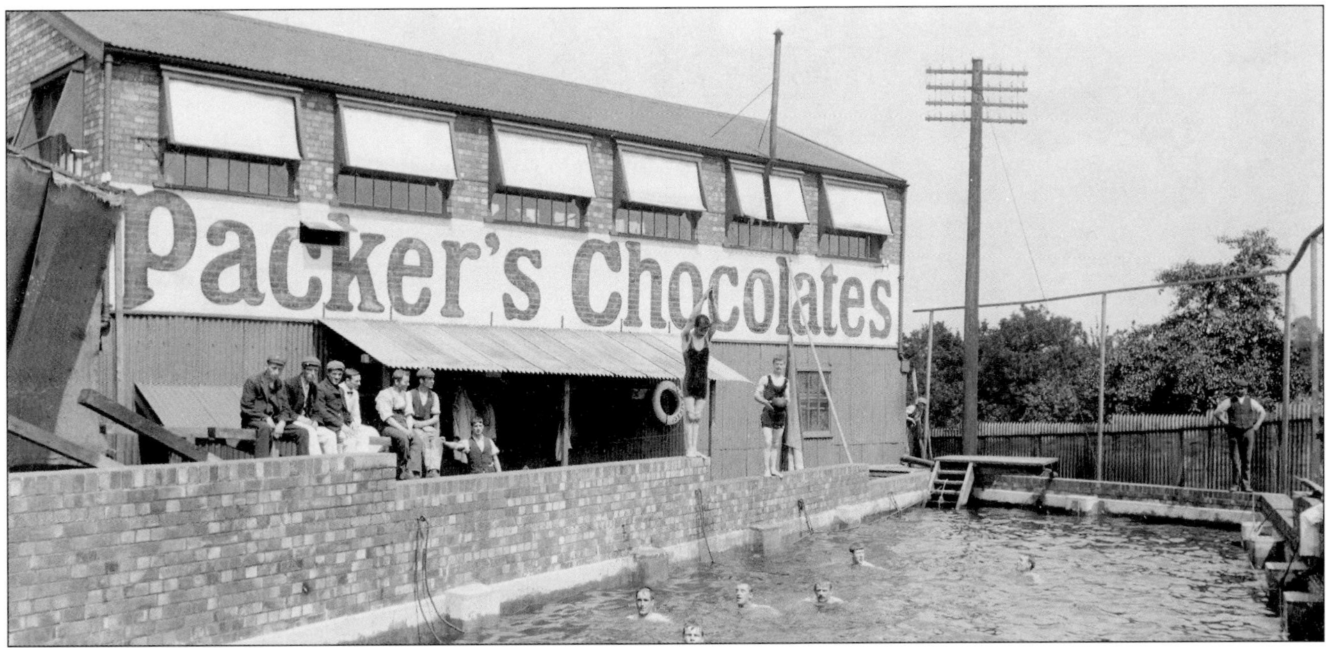

was dissolved in 1885 and it was Burrows who became sole owner of the business.

During 1886 Bruce Cole, then 24 years old, who sold Burrows the occasional hundredweight of sugar borrowed £1,000 from his father to buy the businesses from Burrows. The actual price paid was £950 for all plant, stock, book debts and goodwill.

It took five years before the business came into profit, but by 1896 the business began to take off. The house next door was bought, then the next and the next, and then the gardens were built over. Later another house was purchased in Orange Street.

By 1901 the company had grown to such an extent that a new factory was commissioned at Greenbank in the Easton area of Bristol. The factory was built to the most modern standards of the day and included one of the very first sprinkler systems installed in a confectionery plant in Europe. The construction of the three factory blocks was planned largely by Bruce Cole's brother Horace who had joined the firm in 1900; the first steam engine there was fired up in November 1901.

The business grew steadily and between 1903 and 1912 sales increased by 250 per cent. More investment capital was raised in 1908 when the firm became a limited company.

Throughout the 1920s and 1930s the company was very successful, employing up to 2,500 at its peak. However over the next 20 years the company declined and was eventually bought by James Goldsmith in 1964. It was now renamed Cavenham Confectionery and began a new period of growth.

It was during the Cavenham period that the Elizabeth Shaw business was acquired in 1968 and added to the range of products produced in the Bristol factory.

Elizabeth Shaw had been founded as a confectionery business in 1937 by Elizabeth and Patrick Joyce.

During the early years of the Joyces' marriage they had fallen on hard times and were forced to move in with one of Elizabeth's sisters and her husband - the Bellchambers. Elizabeth had always enjoyed cooking for the family, especially making treats such as chocolates. One of her favourites was a chocolate made from honeycomb crisp which was mint flavoured, developed from a recipe given to her by an American friend. In 1937, keen to help her husband and pay their way, Elizabeth started to produce both Mint Crisps and Langes de Chat - Cats' Tails - on her sister's stove to sell in her brother-in-law's shop. Soon Patrick and Elizabeth had to create a name for these delicious chocolates. After some thought they decided to

Top: *The Swimming Baths of Packer's Chocolates, 1906.* ***Above:*** *HRH Queen Mary, visiting the decorating department.*

combine Elizabeth's name with the name of Shaw from the name Page & Shaw, Patrick's former employer.

As sales increased so did the need for proper production facilities. In 1938 a small kitchen was set up in premises at the rear of 25, High Street, Teddington; soon even that was too small and in 1939 they moved to their own factory - The Mint House in Commerce Road Brentford - and in 1953 to larger premises again in Camberley.

Other products were also marketed under the Elizabeth Shaw brand including Digestive Mint Creams which were, and still are, supplied to the Royal Family; it was that association which led to the granting of the Royal Warrant as a supplier to her Majesty the Queen in 1963, an honour which the company holds to this day.

Alas a disastrous fire swept away the Camberley factory and as a result of the subsequent financial difficulties the company was sold and in 1968 the Elizabeth Shaw brand name and production was moved to Bristol.

The Famous Names range of liqueur chocolates was launched in 1966 and remains a core brand of the business. Famous Names is the number one liqueur chocolate brand in the UK. Between 1981 and 1991 the company changed hands four times being acquired in 1990 by the Leaf Division of Finnish multinational Huhtamaki.

A number of other significant developments took place in the early 1990s including the rise of Elizabeth Shaw Mint Crisp to a 10 per cent share of the UK mint market and the successful launch of Elizabeth Shaw Liqueur Truffles.

The year 2000 saw yet another change of ownership with a management buy out led by Managing Director Malachy McReynolds, Bill Williams (Marketing & Sales) and Paul Keith (Operations) with Chairman Martin Pearce.

Now employing over 150 staff the company enjoys an annual turnover of £10 million including exports of £750,000 and still manufactures its own chocolate couverture to its own closely guarded recipes. The opening years of the new century now sees the launch of new products such as Vodka Shots and Mint crisp Truffles and the reintroduction of Orange Crisp and Coffee Crisp.

The business has come a long, long way from that back kitchen in Stapleton Road.

Top left: *Office workers pictured in 1948.* ***Top right:*** *A view inside the packaging department in the 1960s.* ***Bottom left:*** *The famous Elizabeth Shaw Mint Crisps.* ***Below:*** *A visit from HRH Princess of Wales in 1991 delighted employees and local residents.*

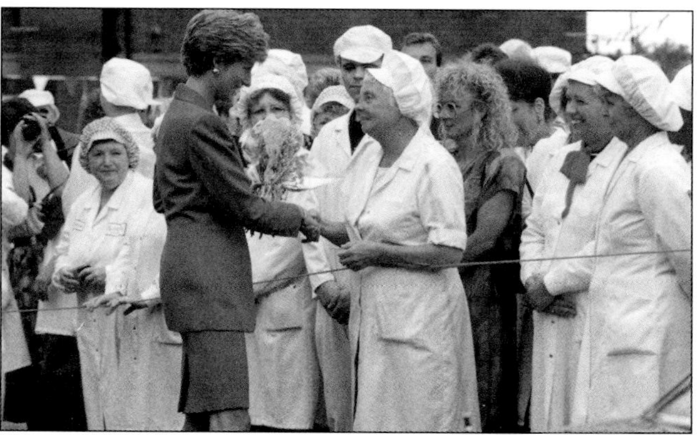

Moulding the future

Ray Engineering had its beginnings in 1923 in an amalgamation of two small companies operating from the same premises at 24 Frogmore Street. Robert Joy's REJ Engineering Co. had already been listed there since 1921. In 1923 Raymond St Clair Carter and Ray Engineering Co. joined them. Initially the two companies co-operated by sharing water and electricity via holes drilled in a partition wall.

The two companies jointly produced the Joylight engine described as the 'outcome of 15 years experience in the construction and design of internal combustion engines'. It was specifically designed for electric lighting in the home. The Joy family also had a garage business, Joy & Co. Motor Engineers in Longmead Avenue, Horfield and had produced a prototype vehicle called the Joy Car.

In 1928 the company moved to premises in Southmead Road named the Waterdale Works. The company acquired a parcel of land between a Church of England Mission Hall and a Police House. The premises were built by Robert Joy; as his family was also involved in the house building business it wasn't very surprising that the factory actually looked like a house.

In that year the company was listed as producing switchboards and switch gear. The handful of workmen could however only be employed for three and a half days per week and times were very hard.

The company did though also have the services of a part time salesman called John (Jack) Evans who worked from premises at 53 Queen Square. From there he represented several different British companies and travelled round England in an Austin Seven.

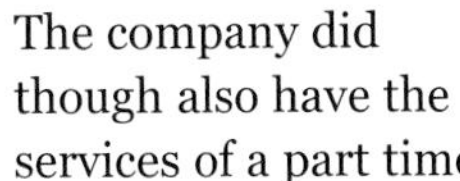

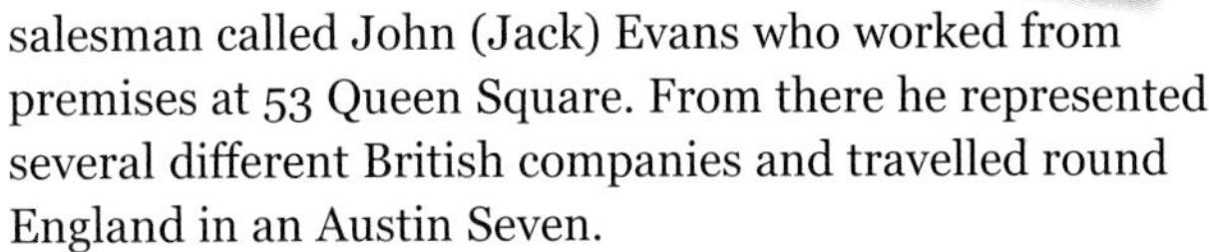

By 1935 things had improved to the extent that the company could offer apprenticeships. Five of those taken on that year would still be meeting almost 70 years later: Mervyn Joy (a nephew of Robert Joy) Eric 'Eggy' Wills, Eddie 'Blondie' Thomas, Geoffrey 'Claude' Meech and

Above: *REJ & Ray Engineering catalogue from 1926.* ***Left:*** *Eric Wills pictured with two 'office lassies' (Bob Joy's Bullnose can be seen in the background).* ***Below:*** *Ray Engineering 1936-1937, Robert Joy pictured third row down fifth from the left.* ***Below left:*** *Mervyn Joy, 1938, working on a Fay & Scott lathe.*

Arthur Ogborne. Each apprentice was indentured to the company for four years: the contracts stipulating 'he shall not haunt taverns or ale-houses!'

Jack Evans who by this time had become Sales Manager regularly made visits to the British Industries Fair at Castle Bromwich. It was during one of these visits that he noticed a stand promoting products made in Derby such as Rolls Royce Engines and Qualcast Lawnmowers.

Although Bristol was known world-wide for industries such as aircraft, printing, chocolate and tobacco, engineering had largely been ignored. Jack Evans felt let down by his own city.

On March 5th 1936 Jack Evans sent a letter to 40 Bristol firms outlining his ideas for some type of association and 12 responded. Directors of nine local engineering companies attended the first meeting. The association became known as BEMA (Bristol Engineering Manufacturers' Association). The speaker at that first meeting was Bob Joy, Ray Engineering's chairman, who discussed power drives. Over the following years the company supplied many speakers on subjects such as metal spraying, plastic moulding and the maintenance of electric pumps. The association still exists today.

Ray Engineering's diverse product range was probably what helped it to survive over the years. Apart from being a manufacturer of switchboards it dabbled in many other areas. Back in 1927 Bob Joy had purchased

a small hand press for moulding with Bakelite. He realised that plastics would be the future - although the machine sat unused in the factory for a further two years! As nobody else was producing plastics at this time Dickie Hughes, the man assigned the dubious task of moulder, had to make things up as he went along! This was the start of today's plastic moulding business, although at the time the firm was content just to manufacture the handles and knobs required for its switchboards.

During the war years many employees were exempted from National Service and a special 'Ray' badge was issued to spare them the stigma of not being in uniform. All engineers - lathe operators, turners and moulders were retained to produce electrics and switchboarding

Top right: *Examples of switchboards from the 1960s.* ***Top left:*** *John (Jack) Evans.* ***Above:*** *Advertising used at exhibitions and in catalogues.* ***Left:*** *An advertisement from 1945.*

for the war effort. It was during this period that the company gained its trade name. The MOD already had a plastics supplier called Ray so the company was unable to use this name. It decided instead to adopt an abbreviation of the whole company name: they branded their products with 'RENCOL'.

Gradually the business expanded and in 1949 Ray Engineering produced its first comprehensive catalogue of plastic moulded machine parts. The catalogue boasted - 'we have been able to produce mouldings as fine as 0.0005 of an inch and our experience as mechanical engineers of 25 years standing has allowed us to offer advice on the satisfactory replacement of metals by plastic'.

Brian Greeves who had links to the Cadbury and Fry families bought the company in 1963 from Bob Joy and the directors of the time, Jack Evans, Tom Leitch, Amy Priest and Mat Southway. Brian Greeves quickly became immersed in the production processes. He used the company's healthy bank balance to finance a major factory overhaul, replacing ageing compression presses

with the most modern injection machines. One of the redundant presses is now housed in the Industrial Museum. It was Greeves who would give the company its competitive edge by pioneering multi-cavity tooling, the ability to mould several different parts in one 'bolster'. During this period, and the brief ownership by Bluemels Plc of Coventry which acquired the company in 1971, Ray Engineering also began to supply aluminium die-cast steering wheels. From the late 70s to the early 90s the company developed a separate fasteners business called Rencol Tolerance Rings. This was eventually sold and is now a successful business in its own right.

Today the Ray Engineering company is still thriving as a plastic injection moulder, and its core business is the production of knobs, handles and hand wheels. Its customer base is diverse as are the applications for which the products are used. A large proportion of components are exported world-wide.

Ray Engineering prides itself on its ability to supply the volume user as well as produce one-off components. As the company also produces its own tools in-house the customer can often gain valuable advice at the design stage in order to produce the most suitable and cost effective components.

By the early years of the new century the firm was being run by a management buy-out team for the second time since the beginning of the 1980s. All the members of the team had been employed by the company for the greater part of their working lives and were a reflection of an extraordinarily workforce, many of whose parents and grandparents had also worked for this remarkable Bristol business.

Top right: *The front cover of a 1949 plastics catalogue.* ***Above left:*** *A view of the factory in 1967, with new Transojets and Compression Presses in the background.* ***Left:*** *Brian Greeves (left) with Arthur Ogborne in the works factory, 1977.*

Hard wearing hardware

Fireguards and cinder sieves; stair rods and clothes boilers; enamel baby baths and breadbins. Many of those reading this book will have memories long enough to recall some of these items which were once common in every household. It doesn't take much mental effort to recall the days when mother still did her washing by hand. But where did all these goods originate?

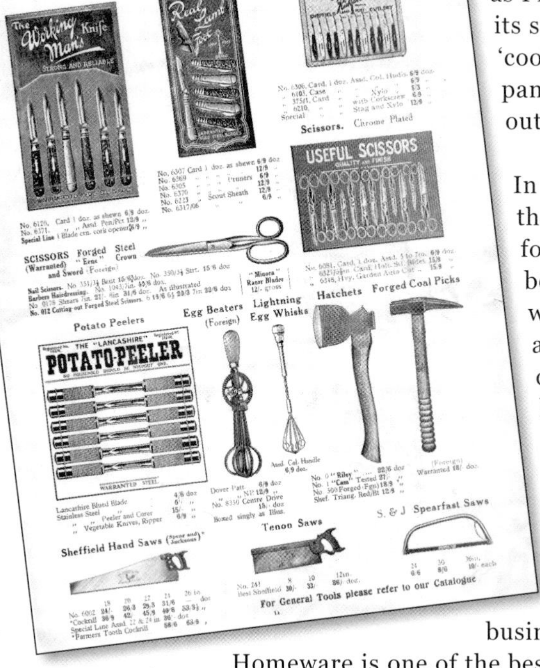

Horwood Homewares Ltd was founded in 1896 by William Joseph Horwood in Queen's Lane premises only a few miles from its current headquarters in Avonmouth Way.

Selling wholesale hardware, enamel-ware, ironmongery, tools, mats, rugs, brushes, glass and china the firm's early catalogues are a cornucopia of nostalgia featuring thousands of objects of delight from chandelier chains, mangles, galvanised buckets, japanned tin trunks and toasting forks to washboards and chamber pots. By the 1930s the firm's catalogue was a hefty 100 pages long.

It was not however until 1935 that the business was incorporated under the name of WF Horwood Ltd. Any optimism for the future heralded by the new name however was premature. During the second world war the firm's premises were almost completely destroyed, with only one of its four warehouses surviving the bombing.

After a short spell in a Nissen hut in Whitchurch Street however new headquarters were completed in 1956, in St Thomas Street, close to the original buildings.

Top left: *William Joseph Horwood who founded the firm in 1896.* **Above:** *A page from a 1950 catalogue showing some very up to the minute (for the time) electrical items.* **Right:** *An example of the Stellar range of fine cookware from Horwood's 2001 range.*

The business still continued as a family owned firm until 1977 when it was acquired by Cowan de Groot, later known as Glenchewton plc.

By the mid 1990s the firm had achieved phenomenal success against such rivals as Prestige and Meyer for its stainless steel 'cookware' - or pots and pans as we know them outside the trade.

In the first five years of the 1990s sales increased fourfold from the beginning of the decade with the Stellar, Judge and Horwood ranges of quality cookware, knives and kitchen accessories selling phenomenally well.

Today after more than a century in the wholesale hardware business Horwood Homeware is one of the best known names in Britain and its famous cookware is rightly known as 'the Choice of Professionals'.

Chocolates?...Yes, Guilbert's

Guilbert's handmade chocolates and confections have been popular with the people of Bristol for generations. The business was started in 1910 by a Swiss exile named Guilbert who had been a chocolate worker in Switzerland.

The original shop was at 40 Park Street with a small factory behind it where the proprietor made everything himself. In those days the equipment and materials differed little from today's, with the exception of silicon moulds for the creams which would eventually replace an earlier rather messy starch process. Guilbert kept the business for only some 10 or 15 years before selling it.

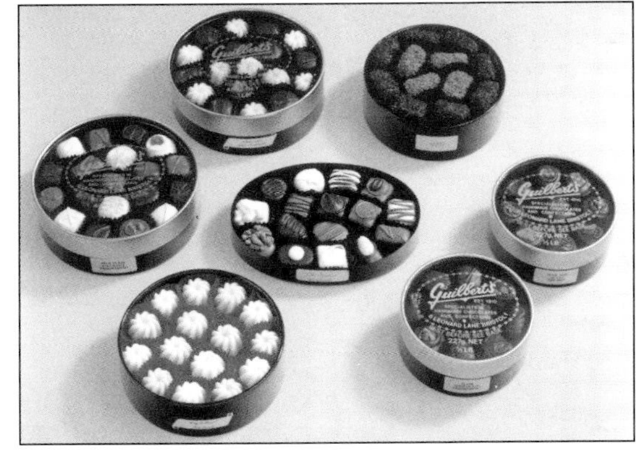

Expansion followed with Guilbert's opening a similar operation at 29 Milsom Street in Bath. A shop at The Promenade in Gloucester Road, Bristol also followed in the late 1950s but this was not a success.

The firm remained in Park Street into the 1950s. The business moved in 1958 to its present address 6 Leonard Lane, a property then owned by the Stride brothers who owned a large number of the properties in Bristol including most of the buildings in Leonard Lane.
Guilbert's had seen a number of owners over the years but in 1953 Frank Haycock came down from Nottingham where he had been involved in a similar business.

When Frank and his wife Betty arrived Guilbert's was then owned by a London firm which was itself a subsidiary of an import/export company.

The owners were not interested in Guilbert's as it was making very little money and Frank took the opportunity to buy the business; he managed to persuade the Stride Brothers, the landlords, to go into partnership with him.

Today's proprietors are Alan and Wendy White. In 1980 Alan White left school and came to work at Guilbert's. Wendy Baugh who was later to become Wendy White started work at Guilbert's in 1981.

Alan became manager and eventually went into partnership with Frank and Betty Haycock in 1988. When the Haycocks retired in 1999 Alan and Wendy became the latest owners of Guilbert's historic confectionery business selling handmade chocolates to a clientele as appreciative today as it was back in 1910.

Above: *Some of the handmade chocolates that Guilbert's produce.* ***Below:*** *Making handmade chocolates in 1958 at the firm's current premises.*

An all round education

In 1858 Mrs Badock of Clifton, Bristol, started a small private school for girls in Burlington Gardens. Even then, it could be described as 'different'. It was unusual in those days for a gymnasium to form part of the buildings, and for Victorian young ladies to wear gym-slips!

Mrs Badock ran her school very successfully for nearly forty years, when she handed her headship over to a friend and ex-pupil, Miss Bartlett. The school had in 1868 moved to Badminton House in Clifton Park, and as the number of girls increased, still larger premises became necessary and they took over three houses in Worcester Terrace.

It was Miss Bartlett's firm conviction that, in the words of Bacon, 'the end of all learning should be the glory of God and the relief of man's estate'. As a practical confirmation of her belief in this ideal she suggested that the School and Old Girls might support a cot in the Children's Hospital. This was taken up and £25 every year was sent, raised by various means. Thought for others has always been a keynote of life at Badminton.

In 1911 Miss Beatrice May Baker, then aged 35, and her great friend Lucy Rendall arrived from Cardiff High School. Beatrice Baker gained the reputation for being something of a new broom and introduced changes which provoked outrage in the minds of some of the staider parents, but doubtless the girls themselves were glad to be free of 'Sunday hats' and 'stays'. Her own dress also caused something of a sharp intake of breath, she eschewed the neat skirts and blouses of her predecessor and favoured free-flowing clothes.

Miss Baker (or BMB as she was universally known) was a great believer in the League of Nations and did a great deal to educate the girls in world affairs. One of her stated aims for the school was to inculcate an ideal of service. She also sought to impress upon the girls the duty of simplicity in dress and living and the true use of money. To encourage an international outlook, girls went on several school trips and there was an interchange of teachers and students from other countries. The school also 'adopted' foreign children under the 'Save the Children' scheme.

***Top left:** Mrs Badock with her sixth form, 1866. **Above right:** The old swimming pool, formerly a sheep dip, opened in 1926. **Right:** BMB, standing centre, with her staff at The Tors, Lynton during the second world war.*

During the 1930s the school removed itself to Lynmouth. During this time Iris Murdoch was a student, serving also as Head Girl. A Peace Conference was arranged by the School at which Indira Ghandi, a former Badminton student and personal friend of BMB spoke.

At the earliest opportunity the school returned to Bristol, and the enormous task of cleaning up the buildings to make them usable as a school again began.

BMB was succeeded by B M Sanderson in 1947, who served as Head Mistress until 1966. She was a worthy successor to BMB, continuing many of the Badminton traditions established under the great lady, but making her own particular contribution to the school, something which is true for all successive Heads, Clifford Gould (Head, 1981-1997) and the present post holder, Jan Scarrow, who took up the reins in 1997.

The school places great emphasis on realising a girl's full potential through the curriculum and other activities offered there. Academic standards are high and girls are expected to work and to achieve. In a relaxed, yet purposeful and stimulating, environment girls are well taught, challenged and enabled to excel in many areas including music, art and sport. They do not just gain first rate results but develop into thinking and independent young women.

Girls are educated for the outside world. This means not cooping them up but giving them as much access to Bristol and all the advantages of a university city that can be safely managed. The School believes it is important for interests to be pursued for their own sake and that learning to take responsibility for one's own actions and appreciate that life is not always organised on one's own terms are lessons just as important as formal classes in a broad education. Girls gain the valuable maturing experience of being independent, having numerous opportunities to test themselves in a lively and adventurous environment, and to excel, not just in achieving first-rate results, but in developing as whole people.

__Top:__ Northcote, home to Badminton School since 1923. __Above left:__ The Junior School Choir. __Right:__ The current headmistress and some of the senior school pupils, 2000.

Pill packing progress

Do you recall the days when every pill came loose in a brown glass bottle rather than in one of those modern childproof containers? And now, more often than not, our pills come individually wrapped in bubble packs whilst hospital supplies of every kind come cocooned in sterile packets. But who makes all those modern wrappers and packages? An awful lot of them are made in Bristol.

Rexam Medical Packaging is the world's leading specialist manufacturer of healthcare packaging materials. The company has manufacturing facilities in Europe, the USA, Latin America and Asia, and it supports its customers with a world-wide network of sales offices.

Locally Rexam is notable for its 13 acre site in Winterbourne Road, Stoke Gifford, a location which when it was newly opened in 1995 was described as the finest medical packaging facility in the world.

But the Rexam story in Bristol goes back much further than the 1990s. Indeed the story goes back to 1844 when 27 year old Elisha Smith Robinson set up a modest business in wrapping paper and paper bags in Baldwin Street. Robinson was an exceptionally hard worker: he cleaned his own windows, swept the floor and polished the brass. He also knew how to manufacture and to sell, and, perhaps more importantly, when and how to delegate responsibility.

By 1846 the business had made such good progress that larger premises were taken in Redcliffe Street, premises which would remain the company's headquarters for decades to come.

Above left: *Founder of the Robinson Group in 1844, Elisha Smith Robinson.* ***Below:*** *A 1929 view of Robinson's letterpress machines.*

When in 1848 Elisha took his brother Alfred into the firm the business became known as ES & A Robinson, a name which would exist for far longer than the brothers.

By the 1960s ES & A Robinson Ltd would be the principal company in the Robinson Group of some 30 separate companies in the United Kingdom, Canada, South Africa, Zimbabwe and New Zealand with assets of £30 million and more than 13,500 employees. It would produce over 100 million finished items of packaging each week, not just paper bags and envelopes but all types of folding boxes, cartons and tubes. The group's prominence was amply demonstrated in 1961 when Redcliffe Street was redeveloped and a prestigious new head office, a 200 feet high office block, was erected on the old site and clad in white marble quarried in Italy. Nor was that the only symbol of the firm's eminence: a company aeroplane, a De Havilland Heron was acquired to ferry company executives and technicians to anywhere in the UK or Europe.

All the production was carried out in eight factories located in or near Bristol, with a total floor space of 1 million square feet and employing 4,000 workers.

By the 1980s the main production site for what was by then DRG Flexibles was its large factory at Fishponds from where Robinsons had operated since 1928.

DRG had become a broad flexible packaging group producing packaging material for a range of end uses, mainly food, though the company had gradually started to produce packaging for the healthcare market, and indeed it had already invented some of the products still made today.

DRG was taken over by Pembridge in 1989 and Bowaters in 1992 with a name change to Rexam in 1996. It had become clear to the company in the late 1980s that to grow in healthcare packaging it would have to invest in 'clean' manufacturing facilities. The company decided to do so, and rather than create separate facilities on current sites in Bristol determined to build a new factory at Winterbourne Road, one which would be a showpiece site for the manufacture of healthcare products. The new site would be as large as six football pitches and longer than HMS Ark Royal with a production area of 7,000 square metres.

The Winterbourne site was a huge investment for Rexam and demonstrated its commitment to the healthcare market. The new production facility would include film co-extrusion, gravure and air knife coating, printing and adhesive lamination; that investment would continue with a new one million pound laminating machine being installed in the early part of the new century. The business had come an awfully long way from selling paper bags in Baldwin Street!

Left: *Hi-tech medical packaging.*
Below: *Rexam company headquarters.*

The current of change

In today's modern world, we switch on the lights or television without a second thought - but, without electricity, where would we be?

The first recorded public display of electric lights in Bristol was on 10 March 1863 when a grand ball and supper was held at the Victoria Rooms to celebrate the marriage of the Prince of Wales to Princess Alexandra. The following year electric arc lights were fitted to the top of each pier, and on the bridge itself, to celebrate the opening of the Clifton Suspension Bridge.

It was however not until 1879 that the Pyramid Electric Lighting Company first put up electric lights at Bathurst Wharf and Prince Street Bridge.

There were no power stations then as we would later come to know them. Early experiments involved using a small steam engine to drive a generator.

In 1893, following a limited experiment in 1882 to light the town centre, when just seven street lights were installed by the Brush Electrical Company using a 12 hp gas engine installed at the bottom of Broad Street, the first permanent supply of electricity was provided by the local council. In that year 20 miles of cable were laid connecting just 120 consumers and 90 street lamps. By 1900 128 miles of cables had been installed leading from the Temple Back Power Station.
The Bristol Tramways and Carriage Company introduced its first electric trams on a line from Kingswood to Old Market in 1895 and built its own power station outside the city boundaries at Beaconsfield Road St George. The economic advantages of electric traction over horse traction were substantial as the electric trams were faster and more powerful, carrying up to 100 passengers compared to a maximum of 50 in a horse-drawn tram.

Avonbank Electricity Works, as it was then known, was commissioned in 1902 with two 745 kw generating sets. Later known as the Feeder Road Power Station it was kept in commission until 1955.

The world was changing forever. The first electric cooker appeared in 1893 and the electric vacuum

Above right: *First cables being laid in High Street, 1893.* ***Right:*** *The laying of electric cables in Baldwin Street, 1900.* ***Below:*** *Jointers Cart pictured in 1912.*

Fifty-five years of municipal generating ended in 1948 with nationalisation of the industry and the creation of the South Western Electricity Board, whose life would itself come to an end with the sweeping privatisation of the late 20th century.

Following the sale of the electricity supply business in September 1999, Western Power Distribution was created on October 1. The company is responsible for the delivery of electricity to homes, schools, offices and shops across the South West - and has a quarter of a million customers in the Bristol area.

With dedicated local teams of highly trained engineers the company is ready to respond to any problems or faults on the network 24 hours a day, 365 days a year. Each year the company invests millions of pounds in the overhead and underground network, reinforcing supplies and ensuring that the network is ready to rise to the demands of life in the 21st century.

The introduction of new technology in the industry has seen the number of interruptions customers experience fall dramatically, and WPD is committed to adopting the latest working methods and practices to ensure that it maintains its overall goal of providing world class customer service. Indeed today, WPD is proud of the fact that it has one of the best records on network performance and customer service in the UK.

Top: *A view inside the control room in the early 1960s.*
Above left: *Western Power Distribution headquarters.*
Below: *Today, work on live lines enables WPD to reduce the number of planned minutes that a customer is off supply.*

cleaner in 1901 - although it took until 1916 for an electric motor to be added to a washing machine for the first time, and until 1956 for the first spin dryer to be marketed.

Not that such luxuries were available to most people in the early days. Indeed for most households the arrival of electricity at first meant little more than having the luxury of an electric light, a huge improvement on gas mantles and oil lamps. A few far sighted plumbers saw that their days as gas fitters might be numbered and as an insurance policy began going to night school to learn how to wire homes for electricity.

Of course our use of electricity was a little different than today. How many of us still recall irons plugged into light sockets dangling from the ceiling, the wireless before we called it the radio, toasters before they learned to pop up, and round pin plugs?

In 1929, due to ever increasing demand, the new Portishead Power Station would be commissioned some 13 miles from Feeder Road which would send 33,000 volts down cables to Bristol.

Electricity had arrived and with it Electricity House one of the landmarks of central Bristol the building of which had begun in 1936.

The pull of magnetism

Today one of Bristol's highest of hi-tech firms is Redcliffe Magtronics. Established in 1931 by Robert G Hawkins, the Redcliffe Radio Manufacturing and Redcliffe Radio Services companies were based at 69 Victoria Street, Redcliffe.

The company specialised in radiograms and public address systems and was run on a day to day basis by Jack Wright. The business remained in Redcliffe until the second world war when its premises were bombed.

Following the bombing the company, then with around 25 employees, moved to Totterdown, to the former King William pub which had closed in 1940. In 1994, long after the departure of the Redcliffe Radio and Engineering Company, the premises would became the Glasnost restaurant.

During the war most of the company's work was directed to the war effort with an emphasis on transistor technology. The company grew after the war, developing its electronics expertise into specialist radio and radar products. This was very delicate work: staff of the time found themselves having to carry large amounts of coal upstairs to heat the workshops as the gas central heating was found to corrode the products.

In 1958 the company won a crucial underwater technologies contract with the MOD. This was a formative moment in the company's history establishing its first links with Rolls Royce and submarine development .

As the 1960s dawned, with Bob Hawkins still active in the business, and now employing around 150 people, the company had grown so much that it was necessary to move. The site chosen was Emery Road at the top of Brislington Hill.

Following the retirement of Bob Hawkins the firm of Bracknell, Dolman and Rodgers bought the company - Harry Dolman being a well known figure in Bristol football.

Around that time Redcliffe began to move into its niche area of customised research and development. The firm then began to use its electronics expertise in more novel

Above: *Robert Hawkins at the Royal Fort during World War Two.* ***Below:*** *The Bristol Railway Arches Site in 1958 that partially house Redcliffe Radios after the bombing in 1940. The site subsequently became the Dragonara Hotel.*

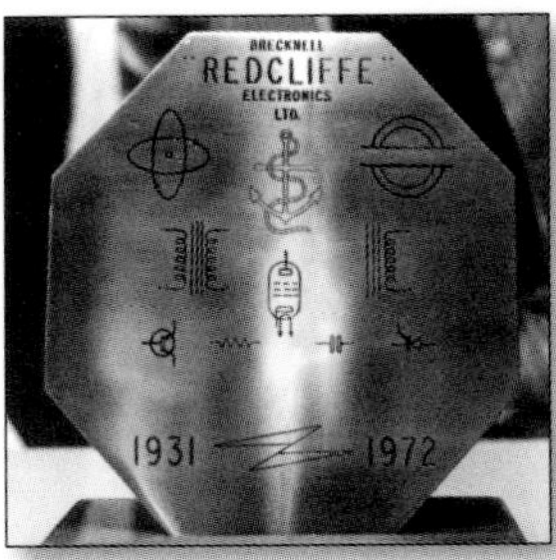

areas including ticket machines for the London Underground. Using the same technology as the ticket machines Redcliffe also developed a roulette and pound note changing machine. This was housed at Ashton Court until tax and gambling laws made it unviable.

When Harry Dolman retired the company came under the ownership of Vokes Filters and was relocated to a site in Pennywell Road. Redcliffe began designing electric circuitry for Vokes' heavy engineering, sewerage and filtration businesses.

The next change for the company came when Vokes was bought by Tillings which split up the different areas of Vokes business. Still employing around 100 staff Redcliffe's electronics core was kept at Pennywell Road and the words 'go to work on an egg' became important: the company was busy designing the wizardry which went into egg grading machines.

In the mid 1970s the company was bought by Highlands and Jack Wright was appointed director. There followed significant changes in the core business of the company as technological requirements shifted from transistors to transformers. At the forefront of technological change Redcliffe began producing hearing aids and intruder alarm systems: at the time both these products were considered very innovative.

Jack Wright left the firm in the early 1980s and the company's association with the 3i group began. Bob Hardy and David Morrison were appointed to lead the company.

Under the new management Redcliffe made its first moves into magnetics. Though few may realise it modern life cannot exist without magnet technology incorporated in everything from computers to microwave ovens. Surprisingly few companies have magnetics expertise, but Redcliffe, building on its early start, quickly became one of the market leaders.

The core defence work had continued since the 1950s but it was not until 1993 that Redcliffe won its first long term contract with Rolls Royce. This brought new levels of security to the company in a highly competitive environment.

In 1995 the company, now at its current location on Clothier Road, Brislington, was taken over by local industrialist Stephen Parsons. Steve's aim has been to develop the magnetics research and solutions side of the business.

A key moment for the magnetics business came in 1996 when Redcliffe bought the Aldershot based company Magnetech increasing Redcliffe Magtronics domestic market share for magnetising, demagnetising and magnet testing equipment from 40 percent to 60 percent.

Today Redcliffe is going through a new period of growth and has contacts and agents across the world; it has come a long way since the 1930s and the days at Victoria Road.

Top left and left: *Robert Hawkins retirement.*
Right: *The Redcliffe Holdings Board - Karl Watkin, Nick Hodges, Dr Hugh Metcalfe and Steve Parsons.*
Below: *Steve Parsons pictured with a NeoDemag.*

Flying metal!

In the 1940s and in the days to which McBraida PLC can trace its origins eyebrows might well have been raised at the thought that a Bristol firm would be using machine tools with distinctly far eastern and Teutonic names like Yamazaki and Gildemeister. How times have changed. Today any engineering firm which does not use such state of the art equipment alongside equipment made by the more familiar names such as Matrix Churchill or Jones and Shipman probably won't be in business very long.

With the second world war making recycling and repairing imperative, and armed with just £150 of capital, Felix Joseph McBraida, an engineering draughtsman, started his then small engineering company. Then the firm was known simply as Associated Tool and Machine Designers. The company became F. McBraida Ltd ten years later in 1954.

The business began at 26A Hanham Road, in a former boot factory, where Felix installed a range of second hand machinery. In 1944 at first there was not even any electricity available at the premises and in addition, because of wartime restrictions, great difficulty was encountered getting the necessary government permit to start the enterprise. At first the main activities were quite simple, metal machining work, reconditioning lawn mowers and constructing trailers.

But mending lawn mowers and minor metal work were not what Felix McBraida wanted to do. Following the end of the war the firm soon found other work. The company developed a close association with the tobacco industry over the years, mostly making parts for the former WD & HO Wills factory during the 1950s.

Felix McBraida retired in 1966 and, at the age of just 27, his son Michael took over completely.

Michael McBraida had joined the company in 1960 shortly after the move to present premises at Bridgeyate, Warmley; his first job was to get Ministry approval for aircraft component manufacture which he did manage to obtain

Top right: *Founder Felix McBraida (front row centre) pictured with all employees including first apprentice Brian Kingston (centre row fourth from the left) and present owner Mike McBraida (back row centre), 1955.*
Below: *Manufacturing in 1959.*
Below left: *Where it all began, 26 Hanham Road, as it is today.*

that same year. The company was soon doing work for aircraft, hovercraft and helicopter companies. The firm even made various parts for Concorde including interchangabilty gauges for Filton and Toulouse in France.

The move to the Warmley premises had been made in 1959 to occupy another ex-boot factory, this time covering some 3,600 sq. ft. By 1964 that area would be doubled, and was increased by a further 75 per cent in 1986.

The company also overhauled cigarette making machines, mostly between 1974 and 1993, including converting cigarette making machines to cigar making.

Most of the cigarette making and tipping machines which were taken from the Wills Bedminster factories to their then new Hartcliffe factory went first to McBraida's for a complete overhaul and upgrading.

McBraida's also overhauled other cigarette machines which were sent to many parts of the world.

The biggest single event in the company's history was in 1971 when Rolls Royce went into receivership owing the firm many months of payments, a major problem which took a long time to recover from.

Despite such setbacks however, by the early 1980s, McBraida could boast 80 employees and an annual turnover of £3 million, with 60 percent of its business being with the aerospace industry including the revitalised Rolls Royce which would eventually sign a long term agreement with McBraida for aero-engine components for its many projects.

Ian McBraida, the founder's grandson and the current engineering director, joined the company in 1986 after training at the guided weapons division of BAe, to become the third generation of the McBraida family to be involved with the company.

Today, unlike the early wartorn days in 1944, the machine shop is equipped with high quality state of the art computer controlled machines. McBraida PLC is now first and foremost a firm of aerospace engineers specialising in precision machining and assembly for high technology industries.

Since its founding the company has achieved an enviable record of steady growth and the resulting stability has ensured its continuing independence. A policy of sound investment and the development of new technologies has been complemented by an enduring commitment to quality and technical excellence whilst a progressive management team has been able to ensure that the high levels of service and responsiveness which were the foundation of the business so many years ago continue to this day.

Top left: *The workshop in the 1980s.*
Above left: *Mike Mcbraida, pictured in 1992.*
Above right: *21st century technology.*
Below: *McBraida's premises pictured in 2001.*

A bridging point for business

It's mysterious stuff: where does it come from and where does it go? Ever since money was first minted, there have been specialists trained to answer those very questions: enumerators, tabulators, tally keepers. Once they kept track using cuts on sticks or marks on clay tablets - now they use calculators and computers but the principle remains the same. Businesses, local authorities, shopkeepers, farmers and individuals all need good financial advice. And where better to get that advice from than a firm of accountants whose roots go deep into Bristol's life.

Today Bristol's Solomon Hare is the largest independent Chartered Accountants practice in the South West, with 24 partners and over 200 staff. As one of the oldest firms in the UK, Solomon Hare is deeply involved with individuals and businesses in the local community. It is a unique accountancy practice occupying a clear and distinctive position in the region with a growing national corporate finance presence.

BRISTOL DIRECTORY ADVERTISING SHEET, 1886. 29A

JAMES & HENRY GRACE,
(J. Thirnbeck Grace. James Grace. Henry Grace, F.C.A.)
PUBLIC & PRIVATE ACCOUNTANTS,
GENERAL AGENCY OFFICE,
ROYAL INSURANCE BUILDINGS,
CORN STREET.

Secretary to the PHŒNIX (BRISTOL) PERMANENT BUILDING SOCIETY.
Agent to the County Fire Office, and Flint & Co.'s British & Foreign Commercial Inquiry Office.

EDWIN J. RICHARDS,
Chartered Accountant,
TRUSTEE IN BANKRUPTCY,
AUCTIONEER, &c.
BRISTOL AUCTION ROOMS,
49, BROAD STREET.

VALUATIONS FOR PROBATE.
Sales of every description of Property conducted.

SOLOMON HARE,
CHARTERED ACCOUNTANT,
AUDITOR, &c.,
44, HIGH STREET.

WILLIAM BOWMAN,
Accountant, Auctioneer, and Appraiser,
TRUSTEE IN BANKRUPTCY,
Estate, House and General Agent, Broker to the County Court, and Tolzey Court Officer,
GRESHAM CHAMBERS, NICHOLAS STREET.

WILLIAM R. NURSE,
Auctioneer, Valuer,
ACCOUNTANT AND ESTATE AGENT,
Agent for the Fire Insurance Association; the London & Lancashire Life Assurance Co.
City Chambers, Nicholas St., Bristol.

C. H. TUCKER,

The entrepreneurial skills of successive partners have enabled it to survive under the same name since the 19th century and it has continually attracted owner managed businesses.

By the millennium, Solomon Hare would be ranked number 22 in the Accountancy league table.

Top centre: *Founder, Solomon Hare.*
Above: *A Bristol directory advertising sheet featuring Solomon Hare, 1886.*
Right: *Alderman Charles Bowles Hare.*

Born in Bristol in 1833, Mr Solomon Hare began working for Bristol accountants, W Bartram in 1860 before succeeding to the firm in 1869. He continued to practice for some years as Hare Barnard and Co. In those early years Mr Solomon Hare worked from his home in Tyne Road, Bishopston and later from his home in North Road. He opened offices at 44 High Street in 1885 from where he advertised himself as a chartered accountant and auditor; he moved home to Cambridge House, Ashley Road in 1889. Some of Hare's earliest clients were the Bristol Tramway and Carriage Company, (now part of FirstGroup) the Gloucester Tramway Co Ltd, John Bartlett and Son Ltd, the London United Tramway Company, Bonds Brewery and the Western Fuel Company. One of Solomon Hare's longest serving clients is Alexandras, who have used the accountancy services since 1928.

By 1898 Mr Solomon Hare, now recognised as one of Bristol's leading figures, was appointed as one of the auditors for the City.

In 1911, the firm was taken over by Solomon's son Edward Hare on his death; Solomon's nephew Alderman Charles Bowles Hare, (pictured below right) another prominent local figure at the end of the 19th century, also had some involvement with the firm.

The offices were moved to Union Street in 1955 and remained there until 1987. Throughout most of the 20th century, the firm continued to provide accountancy services to the people of Bristol in a

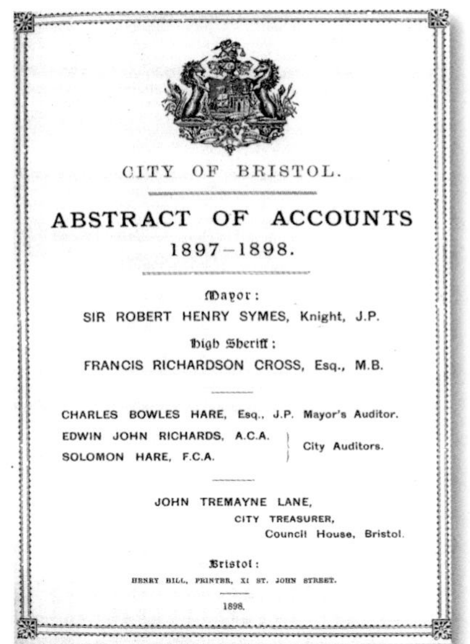

CITY OF BRISTOL.

ABSTRACT OF ACCOUNTS
1897–1898.

Mayor:
SIR ROBERT HENRY SYMES, Knight, J.P.

High Sheriff:
FRANCIS RICHARDSON CROSS, Esq., M.B.

CHARLES BOWLES HARE, Esq., J.P. Mayor's Auditor.
EDWIN JOHN RICHARDS, A.C.A. } City Auditors.
SOLOMON HARE, F.C.A.

JOHN TREMAYNE LANE,
CITY TREASURER,
Council House, Bristol.

Bristol:
HENRY BILL, PRINTER, XI ST. JOHN STREET.
1898.

manner distinguished from that of many other accountancy firms.

By the early 1970s Solomon Hare was one amongst a number of sizeable firms. The accountancy market however grew more competitive around this time, with many small firms being bought up by larger ones, Solomon Hare followed that trend and acquired a number of other firms over a period of more than thirty years: Underwoods was bought in the 1970s, JD Lewis & Co in the 1980s followed by Barkworth & Co in the 1990s.

The firm moved to its present offices in Oakfield Grove, Clifton in 1987.

The rapid growth of the business is impressively illustrated by its annual turnover. In 1970 the figure was just forty-one thousand pounds. Over the next ten years business would increase more than ten times; by 1980 the figure exceeded half a million pounds, by 1990 four and a half million pounds - and by the year 2000 sixteen million pounds was in view.

That huge growth was not however simply due to acquisitions: during the 1980s and 90s the firm had began to expand on its core accountancy skills to offer a range of services, from what would become the Solomon Hare group. The group consists of Solomon Hare Personal Finance, Castlemead Insurance Brokers, Gimlet IT and the Simon Brooke Group. The services within the group range from the traditionals of audit and tax to new services such as Benefit Consulting and HR Services. These new services reflect the demand made by small to medium sized clients regionally and internationally.

Top right: *An aerial view of the Clifton area of Bristol where Solomon Hare's offices are situated.*
Top left: *Certificate of city auditors 1897.*
Below: *Senior Partner, Philip Moody and Managing Partner, David Smart, 2001.*

Reece Winstone Archive

The Archive was so-named by John Winstone following the death of his father Reece, with the intention of carrying on Reece's photographic collecting policy and safeguarding his work. It is the largest and most widely published private archive of Bristol 1840-2000, with 41 volumes to date. In fact through Reece's photography the Archive covers the whole of England, with limited coverage of the remainder of Great Britain and the Low countries. There are presently no personal search facilities and specific enquiries are best put in writing. There may be a charge for searches of unpublished photographs.

Reece Winstone was not only a good photographer but an expert in the darkroom who knew how to provide customers with an excellent service. His well stocked library of glossy 8" x 6" prints was sent out to book and magazine editors by same day post on sale or return. Today

Below: *Reece, by Reece, taken in Queen Square on the afternoon of 9th October, 1948. A new camera with a self-timer on a tubular aluminium tripod may have facilitated this shot; he invariably carried more than one loaded camera.*

many prints are in their self-same boxes, all printed on Bromide paper, glazed and of too good a quality now to pass on. With this second volume of Memories, the original negatives have been directly scanned digitally for the first time, rather than via a print.

Reece Winstone's library, in 1957, began the transformation into a published record and at a stroke Reece literally invented a whole new genre of book - the methodical photographic record of the historic environment. The rest, as they say, is history.

Running an archive is a curious business; ever-expanding (at a slow rate), ever deteriorating (at an uncertain rate) and attempting to keep up with the current concerns of customers. The opportunities to publish the Archive's photographs are limited by funds but in 2001 they are proposing a new volume, No. 42, being an Index of all 7,000 published photographs, together with 12 Maps of Bristol. The various cross indexes in this volume are all electronic. Each photograph is considered and indexed under any of 475 subjects and comes on floppy disk for printing out as the reader wishes via a computer running Microsoft Office '95 or better. The central area Bristol maps are the first edition Ordnance Survey of 1883-85, long out of print, reduced to A4 and printed on art paper. These maps are the best way of finding one's way around pre-war Bristol and for finding the viewpoint of the photographs.

Surveying 120 years ago was nothing if not exhaustive. Take a picture in a back garden before the war and the layout of garden paths and trees can be found on the 1: 500 maps. For those tracing family history or businesses the material is invaluable. Copies of this volume, earlier volumes and prints from the Archive may be obtained direct from Reece Winstone Archive & Publishing, Court Farm, Wookey, Wells BA5 1LE or via e-mail at winstonejohn@lineone.net

Below: *The map of Redcliff, surveyed in 1883 and published at 1:500 scale. It was this area of Bristol with its caves that first drew the interest of Reece Winstone's indexer, Alan Gray. For the family of Reece's wife, Dorothy Attrill, Redcliff was the centre of life. Three generations of Attrill were living in the corner of Georgian Somerset Square (off right) until 1940 (vols. 14/196, 198; 17/76, 81); her grandfather had been employed by the vestry of St Mary Redcliffe, whose vicarage is prominent, centre. Reece saved Thomas Wright's fountain, commissioned by the Duke of Beaufort who had had his townhouse in Somerset Square. He himself grew up in Southville. He used his shot of the Docks seen from Redcliff Parade, top left, as one of the illustrations in JB Priestley's* English Journey *of 1933, when it was re-published 50 years on. 'As it is, it remains a city that was strong yesterday and is still lively today, a city that is old, dignified, historic, and at the same time a bustling modern commercial centre'. By 1983, 50 percent of this map had been redeveloped.*

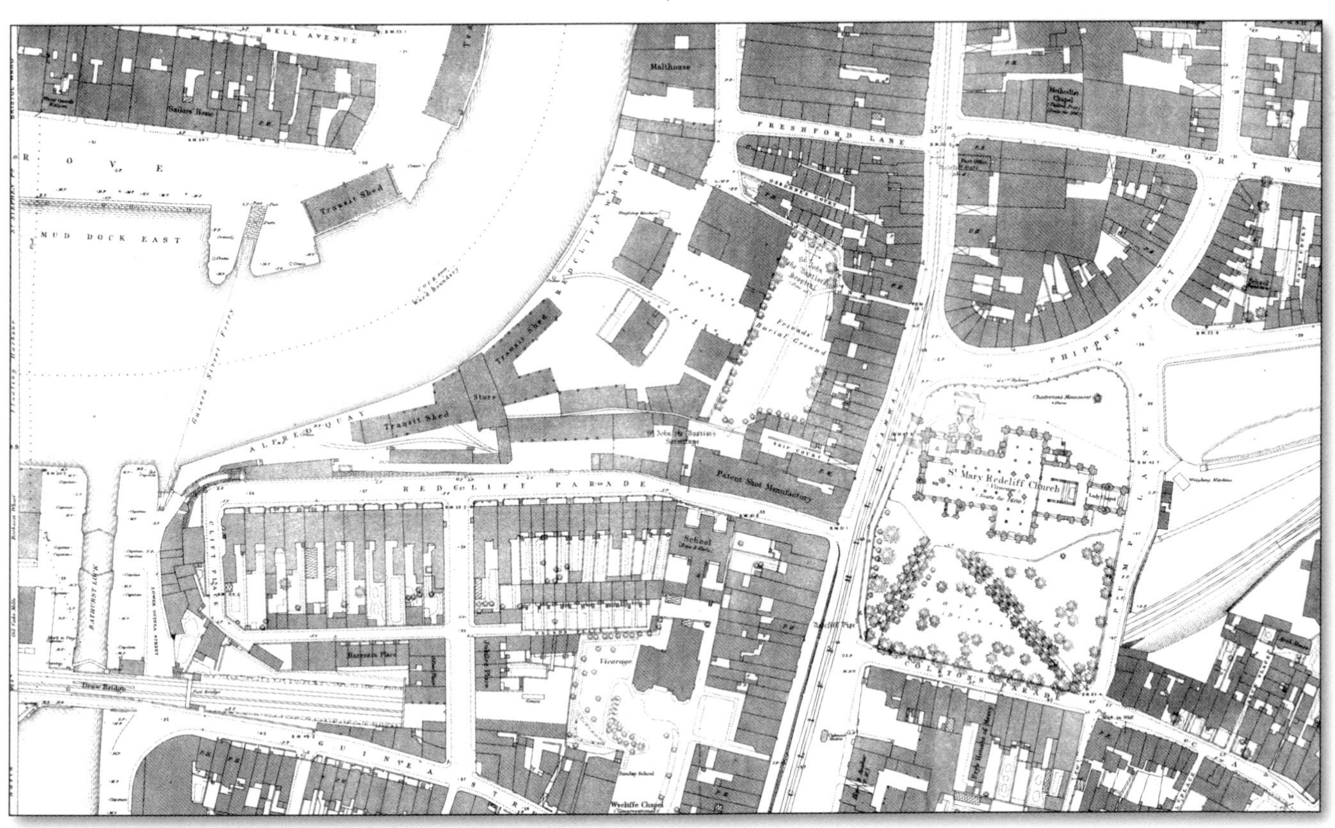

The bus company's booking office on Colston Avenue in September 1949.

Acknowledgments

The publishers would like to thank
Alan Canterbury
The staff at the Central Library, Bristol
Reece Winstone Archive & Publishing

Thanks are also due to
Peggy Burns who penned the editorial text
and Steve Ainsworth for his copywriting skills